The Gift of the Unicorn and Other Animal Helper Tales for Storytellers, Educators, and Librarians

The Gift of the Unicorn and Other Animal Helper Tales for Storytellers, Educators, and Librarians

Dan Keding and Kathleen A. Brinkmann

LIBRARIES
UNLIMITED™
An Imprint of ABC-CLIO, LLC
Santa Barbara, California • Denver, Colorado

Library of Congress Cataloging-in-Publication Data

Names: Keding, Dan, author. | Brinkmann, Kathleen A., author.
Title: The gift of the unicorn and other animal helper tales for storytellers, educators, and librarians / Dan Keding and Kathleen A. Brinkmann.
Description: Santa Barbara, CA : Libraries Unlimited, [2016] | Includes bibliographical references and index.
Identifiers: LCCN 2016002978 (print) | LCCN 2016020869 (ebook) | ISBN 9781440840524 (pbk. : acid-free paper) | ISBN 9781440840531 (ebook)
Subjects: LCSH: Animals—Folklore. | Human-animal relationships—Folklore.
Classification: LCC GR705 .K38 2016 (print) | LCC GR705 (ebook) | DDC 398.24/5—dc23
LC record available at https://lccn.loc.gov/2016002978

ISBN: 978–1–4408–4052–4
EISBN: 978–1–4408–4053–1

20 19 18 17 16   1 2 3 4 5

This book is also available as an eBook.

Libraries Unlimited
An Imprint of ABC-CLIO, LLC

ABC-CLIO, LLC
130 Cremona Drive, P.O. Box 1911
Santa Barbara, California 93116-1911
www.abc-clio.com

This book is printed on acid-free paper ∞

Manufactured in the United States of America

Illustrations created by Lisa Brinkmann Zangerl.

Acknowledgments

I wish to thank Lisa Brinkmann Zangerl for her time and effort in creating the lovely line drawings for the chapters in this book. She patiently listened to my ideas about the art work and made it a reality. Maeve Reilly proofread many of the stories, helping me to improve them. I am indebted to Tandy Lacy, who gave a more thorough edit to the stories. Her background in folktales and in world cultures was invaluable. I thank Betsy Hearne for her insights into the Tibetan tale, "The Young Man Who Refused to Kill." For his support and patience during this project, I wish to acknowledge my son, Daniel. He was always willing to listen to a story and comment or offer suggestions for teacher questions. Lastly, I am grateful to Dan Keding for inviting me to coauthor this work. He has been an excellent storytelling mentor and continues to be a treasured friend.—KB

I wish to thank my wife, Tandy Lacy, for listening, reading, commenting, editing, and indexing the stories; Lisa Brinkmann Zangerl for her wonderful drawings that enhanced our stories and gave them life; Kath Brinkmann who found such wonderful stories and was so patient with my strange ways—she is a wonderful friend and collaborator—and Barbara Ittner who guided and shepherded us with kindness and knowledge.—DK

Introduction

The world of folktales and fairy tales is populated with some of the most memorable characters in all of literature. Among these, many fascinating and fantastic animals stand out. From Pegasus riding through the skies of ancient Greece to Puss in Boots helping a young man on his adventure to General Dog and his army of fellow beasts saving the day for their beloved master, animals have been portrayed as the guardians and helpers of countless men and women on their heroic journeys.

Often the tales of these animal comrades—through their wiles, wisdom, and courage—shed a unique light on the human experience. We see ourselves idealized in the way these beasts guide, aid, and deal with their human charges. Through the guiding paws, claws, and talons of these animals, we understand the proper way to communicate and interact with each other. Their stories are guideposts for our own behavior. Here we find the compassion, loyalty, and wisdom that humans often lack but our animal guides possess in abundance. In this way we are challenged by the animals in these stories to build those qualities in our own lives.

Folktales may be one of the oldest methods of passing down wisdom. There are cautionary tales, wonder tales, historical stories, and *pourquoi* (how and why) tales, to name a few. These stories not only entertain but can inspire deeper reflection and encourage us to explore the world.

The activities in this book are written for learners in grades three through six, designed to enrich the social studies and language arts curriculum as well as programs focused on the environment and appreciation of world cultures. Librarians, storytellers, folktale scholars, and teachers will find these stories and the supporting notes and resources invaluable.

The fascination many children have for wild animals often includes an element of fear. This powerful emotion, without guidance and education, can lead to misunderstanding and even disrespect. These tales feature animals that assist the main character in challenging situations and sometimes save a person's life by sacrificing their own, as in the story from Korea called "The Pheasants and the Bell." The compassionate actions of the animal characters provide a model for behavior and encourage character traits such as respect, generosity, courage, empathy, integrity, and kindness. Teachers may use these stories as a starting point for discussions about human behavior, why some people behave as they do, and why society values certain virtues.

In the classroom, these tales, each with its country of origin identified, can be used to stimulate discussions about cultural diversity. For example, in Asia, dragons are viewed as benevolent—a fact that is clearly illustrated in the story "The Dragons of Ha Long Bay," where these mythical creatures save the Vietnamese boat villagers from the invading Chinese. Studies in biology can be enhanced by stories such as "Yogodayu and the Army of Bees." This tale from Japan can lead into a lesson on how bees benefit humans by pollinating our food crops.

Discussion questions, activities, and additional notes to aid educators are found in the Questions and Activities Section. Readers will appreciate the notes at the end of each story as well as the Story Sources, which include the tale type and references. A separate bibliography offers further reading options. A quick reference table connects the story with the animal type along with the country from which the story originated.

We hope that you will enjoy these stories that span the globe yet hold common themes. Kindness is repaid with kindness: you get what you give.

Section 1

Creatures of the Land

The people believed his threat and with heads bowed, they trudged back to their work. Two soldiers took Maldonado to the woods and trussed her to an ombú tree as though she was food for wolves or wild cats.

Days passed and finally the people begged the Captain to send someone for her body, so that she might be buried. Carrying a black sack for her bones, a group of heavy-hearted people set out to the wilderness. Soon, they found Maldonado tied to the tree. A large puma watched for a moment and then disappeared into the pampas. Maldonado smiled. The colonists were surprised to find her unharmed and well. She told them that the puma and her cubs guarded and fed her but could not free her.

Maldonado was brought back to the settlement where the people argued that she had served her punishment and should be allowed to live in peace. The Captain gave in and Maldonado lived with the colonists for the rest of her life.

The story of Maldonado and the puma spread far and wide. Today, there is a town in Uruguay, neighbor to Argentina, which is named after the kind, brave Señorita Maldonado.

Notes

A weapon made of two stones wrapped in rawhide and tied together with a long rope. It is swung in the air by the rope and the stones serve as weights when it is thrown at the victim.

Pumas are agile cats that can weigh up to 160 pounds and measure 8 feet from nose to tip of the tail. They stand about 2 to 2½ feet tall and have acute vision as well as hearing, which aid in their hunting of prey such as deer, elk, horses, cattle, and sheep, though they will eat anything they can catch. To protect the declining population of this cat species, in 1996, Argentina and other South and Central American countries prohibited the hunting of pumas. The puma is an ancient creature and honored and still active in numerous indigenous cultural groups in South and Mesoamerica.

Buenos Aires was settled by the Spanish around 1536. The city was first founded by a Spanish gold-seeking expedition led by Pedro de Mendoza, on February 2, 1536. In 1539, attacks by the native people forced the settlers away, and in 1541, the old site was burned. In 1580, Juan de Garay from Asunción established a permanent settlement there.

—KB

Oleshek, the Deer with the Golden Antlers

A Sami folktale

It is said that long ago an old man scraped up some dull brown clay and molded it into the shape of a man, and placed the figure in the sun under the south-facing window. Then the old man went inside to help his wife mend a fishing net.

"If you look out the window," he said, "you will see the clay man I made."

The old woman's eyes grew wide as she saw the clay man move. "Oh, what have you done? Now the clay man will come and eat us!"

No sooner than she had spoken these words, they heard stomping sounds as the clay man walked awkwardly toward the house. The door crashed open and the clay man saw the old couple holding the fishing net and staring at him with their mouths wide open in a breathless scream. Grabbing them both, the clay man gobbled them up, fishing net and all.

Out on the street, the clay man saw two girls carrying buckets and a yoke to fetch water at the village square. He snatched them up—buckets, yoke, and all—and then swallowed them whole.

The clay man lumbered down the street where he found three elderly women toting baskets of fresh-picked berries. He ate the three women, berries, baskets, and all.

His appetite knew no end. At the seashore, the clay man scooped up three fishermen working on their boat. He gobbled them up, boat and all.

Turning toward the forest, the clay man tromped on until he came upon three men chopping trees. He devoured the three men, axes, and all.

When the clay man came to a mountain, he looked up to the top where he saw a young deer grazing on tender grass. He shouted, "I am going to gobble you up!"

Now, this deer was no ordinary deer. His name was Oleshek and he was clever.

"Oh," said Oleshek, the deer. "It is a long way up the mountain, clay man. If you stand at the foot of the mountain and open your big mouth as wide as you can, I will jump down the mountain into your mouth. That will be the easiest way to eat me."

The clay man rubbed his dull brown hands together and laughed, "Hee, hee."

He opened his mouth as wide as he could and stood still at the base of the mountain. Oleshek took a short running leap and flew off the mountain, aiming his sharp antlers at the clay man's bulging belly. The clay man shattered into a thousand pieces strewn in every direction. As he broke apart, out came the old man and old woman dragging their net, the two girls with their buckets and yoke, the three elderly women with their baskets of berries, the fishermen and their boat, and finally the woodcutters with their axes. Quickly, they all scattered home.

Later, the two girls brought gold to Oleshek as a gift of gratitude and the men used it to gild Oleshek's antlers as a reminder of his good deed. From then on, Oleshek was known as the Deer with the Golden Antlers.

Notes

Sami, formerly known as Lapps, live on the tundra in the northern parts of Norway, Sweden, Finland, and Russia's Kola Peninsula. Traditionally, the Sami were seminomadic people who herded reindeer. Reindeer meat was an important part of their diet and warm clothing was made from their hides and fur. In Sami mythology, the Daughter of the Sun brought the reindeer as a gift to help the people survive their harsh environment. Religious beliefs of the Sami encompassed shamanism, polytheism, and animism. Sami images of reindeer often depict them flying through the air, sometimes holding a sun disc or a similar sun-related image. In this story, the shiny, gilded antlers and Oleshek, the deer, leaping through the air recall the Sami shamanistic view of the world.

—KB

The Man and the Muskrat

A folktale of the Fipa people of Tanzania

One day a hunter went out with his spear, bow and arrows, and his dog. Because game was scarce, he had decided to hunt farther from his village than he had ever done before.

As he walked, he heard a voice calling out to him saying, "Hunter will you help me over the muddy crossroads? If you help me, I will repay your kindness another day."

The man looked around but saw no one. "Who is it that calls to me?"

"Hunter, it is I the muskrat. Help me now and I will help you another day."

The man turned to look under a nearby bush and saw a little muskrat. "I would help you," the hunter said, "but you stink. You smell so bad that if I carry you across the road I will stink, too."

"Please sir, help me across the road or I will die. If you are afraid of my scent, then use the end of your bow to carry me across to the other side. Someday I will be of great service to you."

The man found it amusing that this little creature thought he could somehow help a mighty hunter like himself. But he also felt pity for the muskrat, and so he scooped the smelly animal up at the end of his bow and carried him across the muddy road.

"Thank you, hunter, for your kindness. Remember, when you need me the most, I will be there to help you," the little muskrat called as he scurried into the bush and disappeared.

That evening the man told his wife about the muskrat. "How could a smelly little rat ever help a hunter of your skills?" she said. And together they laughed and laughed. Soon the muskrat's promise was forgotten.

A few days later the man again went out to hunt. His wife prepared some food for him to carry in case he had to spend the night in the bush.

After traveling a great distance, he finally killed three guinea fowls and turned toward home. But because this was the rainy season, he suddenly saw a great storm approaching. The man knew he had to find shelter for his dog and himself. Luckily, he found a cave, and he and the dog crept into it just as the rain began pounding down.

Now, as it happened, a lion also was hunting in the area and ran to the cave for shelter. When the dog saw the lion, he began to growl. The hunter, trembling with fear, took hold of the dog's muzzle to silence him. Quickly, the man spoke. "Lion, I know that you will eat me but I want you to know that I am a hunter like you, not a thief. I have never stolen food from another family or taken their goods or killed another man. Like you, I feed my wife and children with the game I bring home. Like you, I was hunting for food and came here when the storm struck. Now that you know who I am, you may eat me."

The lion roared until the cave shook with the power of his voice. The man gripped his weapons tightly but the lion roared even louder until it seemed the earth would collapse around them.

"Man, give your dog the guinea fowls to eat. When he has finished, you eat the dog and then I will eat you. Nothing will be wasted."

The hunter was so scared he could not move or reply. The lion roared again. "Did you not hear me? I said feed the guinea fowls to your dog, and when he is finished eating, you will eat the dog and I will eat you."

Before the hunter could answer, the bold voice of another animal echoed loudly from the darkness at the back of the cave. "Yes. Feed the guinea fowls to the dog. When he is finished, you eat the dog. Then the lion will eat you and, after that, I will eat the lion. What do you say my royal bodyguards?"

Suddenly the cave was filled with the loud humming of termites, "Mmmmmmmmmm."

The lion and the man both were shocked into silence. Who was speaking to them from deep inside the cave? Then they heard the voice again. "I said feed the guinea fowls to your dog. Then you eat the dog. Then the lion will eat you and I will eat the lion. What do you say my royal bodyguards?"

The termite army replied, "Mmmmmmmmmm."

Now the lion was thinking more about not being eaten than eating. His roaring had loosened the walls of the cave and bits of rock were falling all around. Thinking quickly, the hunter spoke to the lion. "You hold up the cave so it does not collapse. I will find something to brace it so you can escape the dreadful fate that awaits you."

Confused and afraid, the lion stood up and put his huge paws on the cave ceiling. The man and the dog rushed out and did not stop until they came to their own village.

A few days later the man met the muskrat again. This time the rat told the story of how he had tricked the lion in the cave. The grateful man thanked the little muskrat over and over again. Later, he told his wife the story. Together, they agreed that they would never forget how his kindness to the muskrat had indeed saved his life.

Notes

Lions are the second-largest cats after the tiger. Male lions can weigh as much as 550 pounds. A group of lions is called a pride. The muskrat is native to North America but the name is often used to identify any foul-smelling rodent species. The giant pouched rat of sub-Saharan Africa has been trained to detect mines and unexploded ordinance, saving thousands of lives in war-torn areas. These amazing rats have discovered over 1,500 unexploded land mines in Tanzania alone. Although these rats are three feet long (including their tail) and about three pounds in weight, they are too light to cause the mines to explode. They are also trained to detect tuberculosis and have identified over 5,000 TB patients.

—DK

The Thankful Badger Family

A *Japanese folktale*

Folks who live on Soga-cho Street in the town of Kashihara tell this story, so it must be true. It happened some while ago that a man named Kitabayashi lived with his family in a comfortable old home. To celebrate the marriage of his only son, he gave a feast inviting his relatives, friends, and good neighbors. For the banquet, Kitabayashi and his wife made sure there was plenty of food prepared, especially of *sekihan*—a mixture of rice boiled with red beans, to celebrate the happiness of the newlyweds.

The party went on late into the night. Finally, all the guests took their leave, but still bowls and platters, heaped with delicious food, sat on the table. The tired family decided to clean up in the morning and went to bed sleepy, but happy. In the middle of the night, Kitabayashi suddenly awoke with a start. He sat up from his mat and listened. There was a scraping sound in the next room—an intruder, he thought. Sliding the lacquer door back, Kitabayashi peered at a strange sight. Two large badgers and three little ones sat at the banquet table carefully eating the special dish of *sekihan* with their paws, not spilling even a grain of rice. Indeed, they seemed very hungry and appeared a bit gaunt.

"Ah," said Kitabayashi to himself, "food must be scarce for them. I know how that feels."

Kitabayashi went to bed and told his wife to go back to sleep.

"Let us not ruin our day of joy by denying food to those who need it," he said as he settled back on his mat.

From that day on, Kitabayashi and his wife put food out in the evening for the badger family. One night, Kitabayashi left fish, a favorite food of the badger. It was a full moon and Kitabayashi and his wife watched the badger family gleefully eat the fish with their best manners, not dropping a morsel of food. Then the larger badgers puffed up their bellies and began to drum:

Teketen—Teketen—Teketen
Dokodon—Dokodon—Dokodon

The younger ones sang:

Pom-poko pom
Pom-poko sho

Such was their joy for the fishy treat.

Kitabayashi and his wife smiled. They continued to leave food for the badger family and, at times, his wife even made special tidbits for them to eat.

Then, one moonless night, Kitabayashi heard a noise inside the house. Sitting up in bed, he wondered if the badgers had entered the house. Slowly, the screen door slid open, and a man with a sword stepped inside the bedroom. A second thief followed. The man raised his sword over Kitabayashi and demanded money. Kitabayashi cowered and his trembling wife hid under the blanket. Suddenly, they heard the thud of heavy footsteps. Through the door came two massive wrestlers. One snarled. Quick as lightening, the other wrestler lunged at the swordsman, grasping his arms and twisting them painfully behind the burglar's back until he dropped the sword. The man let out a scream and the second burglar, turning on his heels, fled from the house. The wrestler kicked the sword aside and released his grip. The thief ran away as though chased by demons.

Kitabayashi bowed his head in thanks to the wrestlers but when he looked up, they were gone. With pounding hearts, Kitabayashi and his wife spoke in whispers about the invasion and the strange rescue until, exhausted, they finally fell asleep in each other's arms.

In a dream, the badgers appeared to Kitabayashi and his wife. The badger family bowed deeply to them and the largest badger spoke.

"We come to you in sleep where we can speak our thanks for your kindness. In our time of need when food was in short supply, you saved us from starvation. We are grateful for your generosity. Tonight, we protected you from danger and never will you have to worry about thieves again."

With those words said, the badger family bowed again and Kitabayashi and his wife bowed to their badger friends. When they woke up, they discovered that they both had the same dream.

From that day on, Kitabayashi and his wife continued to leave food for the badgers every night, and they all lived peacefully for the rest of their days.

Kindness will never be wasted in any way.

—Japanese proverb

Notes

Badgers are mammals that will eat almost anything (omnivores). Their short legs and arms are made for digging underground burrows or tunnel systems (called a sett) where they reside. The light-colored Asian badger has dark fur in lines from its eyes to the crown of its head that appear like a mask, similar to a raccoon. Badgers produce a strong-smelling musk to mark its territory. Sixteen distinct sounds, including yelps, growls, churrs, keckers, and wails, are used to communicate with other badgers in the same clan.

In Japan, the badger is known as tanuki. *The lore about badgers was introduced from China, perhaps as early as the eighth century. The shape-shifting badger is considered a trickster-type character, fond of pranks. Not unlike the European fairy, the badger might bargain with a human merchant for goods and pay with gold that later is transformed into dry leaves. In Japanese folklore, the badger can be a vengeful character, a grateful friend, or a mischievous prankster. In the story above, the badger family behaves as appreciative friends.*

—KB

Snake narrowed his eyes and then sank to the ground and slithered on until they found a dog lying in a patch of dry grass. Snake greeted him saying, "Good day, brother Dog."

The hunter asked, "We need you to judge. Is it fair for the snake to bite me after I saved his life by lifting a heavy stone off his back?"

Dog sat up and perked his ears. He scratched his head with his hind leg and said, "How can I judge this without seeing the situation. Where did this happen? Take me there."

The three of them went to the place where the boulder fell upon the snake. Dog said, "Now Snake, show me exactly how you were trapped under the rock." So the snake moved next to the rock and the hunter pushed the large rock to roll on top of the snake's tail.

"Snake," Dog asked, "is this how the hunter found you?"

Snake could not move. "Yesss," he hissed.

"Excellent," said Dog, "now you can wait for the next man to free you."

Realizing he had been tricked, Snake twisted and arched, biting his own tail trying to escape. In his anger he vowed always to strike at Man.

Then the dog turned to the man and said, "You are a hunter and I am a hunter. Let us work together and be friends."

And so it was that Dog and Man became friends. Man will feed his dog and Dog will protect his master. But Snake has never forgiven Man and will bite without mercy. And so it is.

Idan wata ta koni mutum, in ya ga toka sai ya gudu

(Once bitten, twice shy.)

Notes

This story is an example of a pourquoi *tale that explains the origin of something in nature or how something came to exist.* Pourquoi *is a French word that means "why."*

Dogs are the oldest domesticated animals associated with human beings and are thought to have diverged from wolves some 40,000 years ago in the region of Eurasia. Humans benefitted from cohabitation with dogs because of the animal's robust sense of smell that assisted in the success of the hunt. Dogs cleaned up scrap foods around the campsite, provided warmth to humans by sleeping beside them, and acted as guards at night.

—KB

Mighty Mikko

A Finnish folktale

Far, far away in the midst of a pine forest, there lived an old man, his wife, and Mikko, their only son. In early spring, before the flower buds blossomed, Mikko's mother took ill. He and his father cared tenderly for her, but she did not recover. They mourned her passing and, shortly thereafter, his elderly father sickened with the same illness. On his death bed, he spoke.

"Mikko, my beloved son, I have little to give you, only my three snares to catch wild animals. After I pass from this life, go into the woods and check the snares. If you find a wild creature in a snare, release it with care and take the live creature home. Do as I say and all will be well."

After his father's death, Mikko was grief-stricken and lonely. But he remembered his father's words and dutifully trekked out to the woods to check the snares. The first trap was snapped but empty, the second was still set and waiting, but the third held a small, red fox. He rescued the furry creature from the snare and in his arms, he carried the little fox home. After sharing his supper, Mikko went to sleep with the little fox curled up on his bed. Soon, they became inseparable companions.

One day the fox noticed that Mikko seemed lonely and thought it was time for the young man to wed.

Mikko shook his head. "What woman would have me, a poor man?"

The fox scoffed, "You are a strong, handsome young man. You are kind and gentle. What princess would not want such a fine man as you?"

Mikko snorted. The fox said, "Leave it to me. I will arrange a wedding with the beautiful and kind princess of our land."

Off he trotted toward the king's castle. Out of curiosity, the king granted the little red fox an audience.

The fox stood tall and spoke. "Greetings from my powerful master. He requests the loan of a bushel measure."

"Who is your master," the king asked. "Why does he want my bushel measure?"

The fox smiled and whispered to the king, "Surely you have heard of Mikko?"

The fox glanced at the courtiers standing by the wall trying to listen. "Mighty Mikko as he is called by some."

The king did not want to appear ignorant of such an important man in front of his courtiers so he replied, "Oh, of course, Mikko, Mighty Mikko. Yes, of course, he may borrow my bushel measure."

The fox took the royal bushel basket to the woods where he hid it among the bushes. Then, he searched for hiding places where village people kept their savings, in nooks and crannies, in tree roots, or under stones. He found enough silver and gold coins to suit his purpose. Into the cracks and seams of the wooden bushel measure, he stuck the coins. The following day, he returned the bushel measure to the king.

The king saw the shining coins caught in the cracks of the measure and was impressed. Mikko must be very wealthy to be so careless with his treasure.

"I should like to meet your master," the king said. "Please invite him to visit."

Looking down at his feet, the fox hesitated. "Your Highness, I am sure Mighty Mikko would appreciate your kind invitation, but alas, at this time he is in search of a bride so we are preparing for a long journey to visit foreign princesses."

This gave the king an idea. Perhaps this wealthy man might want to marry his daughter. Somehow he must get Mighty Mikko to meet her. Anxious now, he said, "I would consider it a great favor if your master would visit me before he embarks on his travels."

"Ah," said the fox, appearing distressed. "I mean no disrespect but, you see, my master travels with a large retinue and your castle, if you will pardon me, is too small to entertain him."

The king then suggested that Mikko travel with a small group of servants, but the fox shook his head saying, "He either travels with his army of people or he walks disguised as a poor trapper, with me as his only companion."

They agreed that Mikko would come dressed as a woodsman and that the king would provide elegant clothing for him to wear. The plans were made and the guest chambers were prepared for Mikko's visit.

The fox hurried home to share the news. The next day they started for the castle.

From the upper window of the castle, the princess waited until she saw the fox with a robust young man at the castle gate. With her hand on her heart, she smiled at the thought of such a handsome man as her husband. When she met Mikko, now finely dressed, she blushed as he bowed before her. His manners and appearance pleased the king as well.

Mikko impressed the court and royal advisors with his modest demeanor and his good looks. The king's daughter fell in love with Mikko's gentle ways. In a private meeting with the king, the fox suggested the two be wed. After consulting with his advisors and daughter, the king approved, and the wedding was arranged.

Mikko thanked the fox for his efforts but was worried about what might happen next.

"Now that I am happily married, the king will expect me to take my bride to my castle and I have none. What am I to do?"

"Do not concern yourself," said the fox. "I have matters in hand. Leave it to me. Tonight, tell the king it is time for him to visit your castle and to bring your bride to her new home. Just do exactly as I say."

Upon hearing those words, Mikko went to the king. The king was thrilled to hear the invitation, for he was troubled by the thought that he had been too quick to allow the union between his daughter and Mikko without reviewing the young man's holdings for himself.

The next day, the fox instructed Mikko to travel the left fork of the road, which would take them to a splendid castle owned by a wicked old dragon known as Worm. The fox reassured Mikko that he would take care of everything and instructed him to show no surprise along the way. The dragon's castle would soon be his.

"All will be well," smiled the fox, as he quickly headed down the road toward the dragon's estate. As he neared the castle, the fox stopped to talk with some of the workers harvesting crops.

"Excuse me, for whom do you work?" he asked.

A field hand replied, "We are subject to our master called Worm."

day she came to the outskirts of a city. She heard a party of men hunting birds. Frightened of the approaching hunters, she quickly climbed a fruit tree. The leader of the group, the son of a king, called them to a halt.

"I will rest here for a while," he said and sat down under the fruit tree.

The woman silently wept and her tears fell upon the prince. Looking up, he saw the beautiful young woman.

"Why do you cry?" he asked.

"My life is a story too sad to tell," she replied, trembling.

"Come with me to the palace," said the prince. "There you can tell me about your sorrow."

"My brother must not know where I am," she sobbed. "He will hurt me again as he did when he cut off my hand." She held up the arm without a hand.

"I promise no harm will come to you," said the prince. He called for his servant to bring a large cloth. They covered the maiden from head to foot so she would not be recognized and the group headed toward the city.

At the palace, the young woman rested and, after she was refreshed, told the kind prince her story. As he listened, the prince was so taken with her beauty and gentle manner that he became determined to have her as his wife. He told her not to worry about her future.

"I will care for you and protect you," he said.

When the prince went to his parents, they questioned his choice of a marriage partner. They did not know anything about this young woman with no hand whom their son found in a tree. But they loved the prince and bowed to his wishes. The young woman agreed to the marriage and a grand wedding feast celebrated the union. The king and queen found their new daughter-in-law to be kind and gracious as well as lovely. They embraced her and were content. After some time, a son was born to the happy couple and the king and queen rejoiced.

One day, the king sent his son to a region far away to review his holdings. The prince kissed his wife and child goodbye and promised to return as soon as he could.

In the meanwhile, the greedy brother had sold off all of his sister's property and wasted the profits. He continued to spend away his wealth until he was reduced to begging. The villagers despised him and so he traveled to the city of the king where he hoped to beg or trick people into giving him money. There, he heard of the prince's journey and of his beautiful one-handed wife. He realized that the prince's wife must be his sister.

Plotting a story to win favor with the king, the evil brother went to the palace. He told the king that his son's life was in jeopardy. The one-handed woman was really a witch and every man she married, she killed. She had been driven out of village after village and one group had chopped off her hand in punishment.

"The prince is in danger. You must kill her before she harms your son!" the envious brother exclaimed.

The king was torn. His daughter-in-law had been nothing but good and kind. Still, they did not know anything about her. "Perhaps," thought the king, "it is true. I cannot risk the life of my only son but I will not kill her."

So the king ordered his soldiers to force the woman and her child from the palace and out of the city. The young woman did not know what she had done but fled to the bush carrying only her son and an earthen pot. There, she stopped to rest, wondering what would become of her and her small son.

Suddenly, out from the grass came a snake. "Please," it said, "hide me in your pot. Save me from my enemy!"

The woman, without thinking, turned the pot over and tilted the rim so that the snake could coil up inside it.

"Save me from the sun and I will save you from the rain," whispered the snake.

The young woman did not understand but when she turned around, she saw another serpent sliding swiftly through the grass, his head arced, ready to strike.

"Have you seen a small snake pass by?" it hissed.

She pointed away from the pot in another direction and the serpent moved on with great speed. When the serpent was gone, she lifted the pot and freed the snake.

"I thank you for saving me," said the snake. "Where are you going and why are you and your child alone in the forest?"

The woman told him her story and he said, "I will take you to my home where you will be well-received. No harm shall come to you. You saved me from the sun and I will save you from the rain."

The woman and the snake traveled for some time until they came to a lake where they could rest and bathe. Suddenly the child slipped into the deep water and the woman could not see him. She cried out and the snake told her to reach into the water with both arms to find him. Panicked, she did not know what else to do, so she waded waist deep into the water and reached down with both arms. Immediately she touched her son. She pulled him up, unharmed, and was astonished to see that her hand had regrown onto her wounded arm. With great joy, she found herself whole again.

"Come," said the snake. "My elders will want to reward you for saving my life."

"This," the woman replied, smiling at her new hand, "is my payment. It is reward enough."

"You saved my life," said the snake. "My elders will want to meet you and thank you themselves. Come."

The woman had no home and no place to go, so she followed the snake until they came to the Kingdom of Snakes. There, she and her child were welcomed and offered every hospitality. The elders thanked her again and again. After some time passed, the woman decided to try to find her husband.

The snake said, "When my parents offer you gold and jewels, ask instead for my father's ring and my mother's carved wooden box."

She did just that. Father Snake gave her his ring, telling her that it would provide food whenever she asked. The carved box would give her clothes or a house upon request. She thanked the snakes for their kindnesses and gifts then walked back into the forest toward the king's city.

Meanwhile, the prince had finally returned to the palace. Fearing to tell the truth, the king told him that his wife and child were dead and showed him two false graves. Weeping, the prince threw himself on the mounds. For days after, he would not leave his room, refusing to eat. The king and queen grew quite worried.

But the wicked brother, who had been richly rewarded by the king and now acted as his advisor, told him not to tell his son the truth.

One morning, the sad prince looked out his window and saw a handsome new house at the edge of the city. His servant told him that the house belonged to a beautiful woman and her young son. This news stirred his curiosity and he announced that he would visit them. When the king and queen heard of their son's intention, they, as well as others, joined the prince as he walked toward the large house.

Now, the woman who lived there was the prince's wife. She had asked for the house from her magic carved box. When she saw the group of people coming to visit, she took out the snake's ring and ordered a feast. As the people approached, the young woman was overjoyed to see her husband, the prince. She flung open the door and invited them to eat. Her husband immediately recognized her and ran to her, kissing her cheeks. He embraced his son who was now a strong little boy.

When all had eaten, the young woman told her story from start to finish. She said, "So you see, it was my own brother who chopped off my hand in his greediness and it was my parents' blessings and the help from the Kingdom of Snakes that saved me."

The king told of how he had been deceived and asked the young woman what punishment her wicked brother should receive.

"Do not kill him," she pleaded. "Send him away, never to return here again."

From that time on, the prince, his wife, and child lived in much joy and happiness. In gratitude to the snakes for their blessings and kindness, the prince commanded that no one in his kingdom should ever kill a snake again.

Notes

In some African cultures, the snake is a symbol of renewal and creative life force because it sheds its old skin and is reborn into its new skin. The snake also is identified with healing, fertility, rain, and the knowledge of secret things. In some areas of Africa, snake worship is part of a long-standing tradition.

Africa is home to many dangerous snakes including puff adder, black mamba, boomslang, python, spitting cobra, and Gaboon viper to name a few. Snakes are legless carnivores that swallow their prey whole and digest them with powerful stomach acids. They smell their prey with their tongue and sense approaching animals through the vibrations in the air and on the ground. The largest snake recorded was a 37.5-foot anaconda from Colombia. The smallest snake is the Barbados thread snake measuring about 4 inches long.

—KB

Blind Man's Bluff

A Russian folktale

Far, far away in Russia, a very long time ago, there lived a peasant with his gentle daughter. In his loneliness, he married a widow who had a daughter as well. Thinking to give her own daughter an advantage, the mother plotted to get rid of her stepdaughter, Anya. So, she began to complain to her husband.

"Your daughter is lazy," his wife griped. "Anya sings instead of paying attention while she spins the flax into thread. You must take her out to the mud hut in the woods. Let her stay there over night to get her work done." His wife nagged and bullied until the simple man finally agreed.

The black mud hut sat deep in the thick forest. It was no place for anyone to spend the night, just a temporary shelter for woodsmen. Anya's father gave her the means to make a fire as well as grain to make kasha porridge for her supper.

"Anya, be a good girl," he said. "Keep the door locked and the fire going. Eat some kasha and do your spinning. I will come for you in the morning." He kissed her forehead and shut the door.

Locking the door, Anya then made a fire. As night fell, she put down her spinning and cooked the cereal to eat. Suddenly, a little brown mouse appeared out of nowhere.

"I am very hungry," it squeaked. "Please, share some of your kasha with me."

Anya gladly gave the mouse as much as it wished, for she felt lonely and was happy to have company. The mouse ate its fill and then disappeared. In the middle of the night, as Anya lay watching the fire, a huge black bear with long claws and pointed teeth forced open the door. Anya sat up, with wide eyes staring.

"I have come to play blind man's bluff," he said. "You will ring the bell in the dark and I will try to tag you. Now, put out the fire and I will put on the blindfold."

Anya stood quaking. The mouse crawled up to her shoulder and whispered, "Tell him you will play, but give me the little bell and I will run around while you hide under the stove."

Anya agreed to the bear's game. She put out the fire and quickly hid under the stove. In the dark hut, the blindfolded bear tried to find the girl, but the mouse led him on a merry chase, ringing the bell and running in circles. Growling in frustration, the bear threw firewood, this way and that way, aiming at the sound of the bell. Finally, he gave up.

"You win," he said. "I will leave your reward by the door."

The next day, Anya's father said to his wife, "I will go and fetch my daughter."

The mother nodded and grinned. She thought he would find nothing but Anya's bones. Later, the family's white dog ran to the gate, jumping up and down in excitement.

"Anya is back with a basket of goodies," the dog said.

"You mongrel, why do you lie?" snapped the mother.

Then she looked out the window. Sure enough, there came her husband with his daughter carrying a large basket. It was filled with good things to eat and a handful of gold pieces. The mother's eyes grew big and she ordered her husband to take her daughter, Nataliya, to the mud hut for the night. Surely her daughter would bring back more than Anya, more berries, more honey, and more gold.

In the forest hut, Nataliya's stepfather gave her food, flint, and the same advice he gave his own daughter. Night came and the girl cooked her kasha. The little brown mouse came out and asked for something to eat. The girl snarled at him.

"Pest," she screamed and threw a piece of kindling wood at him but missed. Then, she gobbled down her porridge. Later, she put out the fire and laid down to sleep.

At midnight, the big black bear forced open the wooden door and called out:

"Hello, little girl! Let's play blind man's bluff. Here is the bell. Run and I will try to catch you."

Then the bear snuffed out his torch. Nataliya's hand trembled badly and the silver bell tinkled in the dark where she stood holding it. The mouse hid and listened to the screaming.

The following morning, the mother sent her husband to the mud hut. "My daughter will have two baskets of good things to eat and money to spend," she declared with a smile.

The dog barked at the gate, "Only bones in the basket."

The mother threw a stick at the dog, "You lie!"

But she saw in her husband's sad eyes that it was true. The basket he held contained bloody bones, all that was left of her only daughter. In shock, the mother tore at her hair and screamed in grief. That night she died of a broken heart.

Anya grew up and married well. Her father lived with her family in peace and contentment.

What you'll go looking for, that you will find.

—Russian proverb

Notes

Farmers consider mice to be pests because they devour the farmer's grain. The root word for "mouse" came from Sanskrit meaning "to steal." Mice are resourceful animals and highly adaptive to any environment. Because of their high level of reproduction, mice are used in genetic research and thus aid humans in medical studies.

"Blind man's bluff" is played in many countries, including Ethiopia, India, Korea, Japan, China, Finland, Italy, Germany, Austria, and France. A version of the game played in the fourteenth century had the seeker, or the person who was "it," blindfolded or wearing a hood over his head while the other players hit at him until he caught one of them.

—KB

The White Spider's Gift

A folktale from Paraguay

Long ago, deep in the thick green jungles of Paraguay, there lived a young man named Pikí and his mother. Every day they collected water in large clay jars at a fresh spring that fed into a wide creek. Pikí always took time to visit with his friend, a white spider, who lived on a yerba maté bush that grew near the spring. The white spider always showed her delight by crawling onto Pikí's outstretched hand and dancing on his palm.

The spider's eight-legged capering brought a smile to Pikí's face, and his mother looked on with great tenderness toward her gentle son and his unusual friend. She remembered the longtime friendship began when Pikí was a child and had rescued the white spider from drowning in the bubbling spring water. Pikí had carefully scooped up the sinking spider from the swirling waters and gently placed it upon a yerba maté bush. Ever since then, the white spider made the bush her home, living on a yellow silken web, its delicate pattern woven between the broad yerba maté leaves.

One day, as the white spider played and danced on Pikí's hand, the young man heard the sound of splashing water. In the creek, two women were paddling a dugout canoe. The younger one was a lovely maiden with soft, dark hair. Pikí could not take his eyes away from her. As they passed, he could see that her brown eyes were warm and friendly. Sitting in the front of the canoe, she paddled with strong arms and a straight back as her aunt steered the canoe from the back.

As the canoe traveled downstream, Pikí sighed aloud.

"She is so beautiful, Mother. Who is she?" he said.

His mother saw that her son was smitten. "Come, Pikí," she said. "Put your spider friend back on her web. We have work to do. I will tell you all about her on the way home."

As they walked home carrying the heavy water jars, his mother told him that the maiden was the chieftain's daughter and her name was Tukira. She had lived with her aunt in a distant village after her mother died but now returned home to marry according to her father's wishes.

Pikí could think of nothing but the lovely maiden. One afternoon, Pikí was gathering *jabuticaba* berries when he spotted the Indian princess. Tukira was gathering flowers to braid into a garland for her hair. She wore a white tunic with a wide purple sash. Taking a deep breath to muster his courage, Pikí greeted her and offered her some of the sweet, ripe fruits from his basket. Smiling shyly, she ate a berry. Soon they were laughing and talking. From that time on, they often spent the hot afternoons together picking berries and swimming in the cool creek. Before long, it was clear that Pikí and Tukira cared deeply for one another.

According to tradition, the chieftain would give warriors, tribal princes, and other strong young men the chance to gain his daughter's hand in marriage. A competition of games was announced, and a husband would be chosen at the end of the contest.

Many a handsome prince, strong warrior, and fine youth competed in the races and hunting contests. Pikí did quite well and, at the end, he was one of four winners. To break the tie, the chieftain proposed that whoever brought the most precious and original gift within three days' time would become Tukira's husband.

Heartbroken, Pikí could not think. He was poor and had no idea of treasures from afar. Tukira saw his distress and told him to pray to the supreme god, Tupá. So, Pikí went to the spring where he first saw Tukira. By the yerba maté bush, Pikí prayed to Tupá with all his heart.

Suddenly, he heard a tiny voice saying, "I will help you succeed. Come back tomorrow morning and I shall have your special gift ready."

The handsome young man looked down to see his eight-legged friend. Surprised, he asked, "How is it that you can speak?"

The white spider replied, "It is by the grace of the god Tupá. Do not worry."

Through the night, the white spider wove her silken yellow thread into a shimmering lace mantle. At its center, she wove the pattern of a passion flower. Surrounding the passion flower, she created delicate orchids and graceful birds to border the edges.

At sunrise, on the last day of the contest, Pikí visited the white spider again. There, at the bottom of the bush, lay the exquisite, delicate lace shawl. Pikí gave thanks to the white spider and to the god Tupá. Clutching the mantle to his chest, he hurried to the village.

The other men had brought fine gifts of rare animal skins, jewelry that sparkled, and a headdress made with colorful plumes and silver ornaments, but as Pikí gently placed the exquisite mantle on Tukira's head and shoulders, the people gasped. She looked radiant.

"Pikí has won!" declared the chieftain.

With drumming, dancing, and singing, the wedding was celebrated. Never were there a bride so beautiful and a groom so happy.

As the years went by, the delicate lace mantle was passed on to Tukira's daughter, to her granddaughter, and each generation after. Other village women tried to weave the intricate patterns with fine threads, but none could match the unique gift of the white spider's extraordinary lace.

Never kill a white spider because they bring money and luck.

—Folklore of Paraguay

Notes

Women of Paraguay make a special lace called ňandutí, *or spiderweb lace that is famous throughout the world. It is an embroidered lace worked on fabric with circular designs inspired by the flowers and animals of the area.*

Spiders have eight legs and are not classified as insects, which have six legs. Without spiders, the insect population would increase, unchecked. Spiders eat vast amounts of pesky bugs that they catch in their webs. Spider's silk is unique because it is 5 times stronger than steel and about 30 times more elastic than nylon. The silken thread they produce comes from the six spinneret glands at the bottom of their abdomens and is made of protein and water. In the average lifetime of a spider, it will make more than four miles of silk thread.

—KB

Section 2

Creatures of the Sky

How the Wasp Lost His Voice

A folktale from Mongolia

Once, a long time ago, Khan-Garid, the great eagle and king of the feathered world and all that fly, sent for Swallow and Wasp. When they arrived, the great Khan said, "I want you to fly around the world and seek out the animal with the tastiest meat. Tell me which one it is and I will only eat that animal for my meals. You have one day to complete this task. Bring me your answers tomorrow evening."

Swallow and Wasp each set out in different directions on their quest. As the sun rose and the day became glorious, Swallow forgot all about Khan-Garid's command. She sang and soared, happy to be free on such a beautiful day. As she sailed over a village, the people below were delighted at her aerial acrobatics and her wonderful song. They clapped and cheered at every swoop and dive.

Wasp, who was very serious and extremely hard working, was busily carrying out Khan's order. Leaving a trail of stings and pain as he flew, the Wasp tasted the blood of every creature that he came upon. After all, he was a disagreeable fellow at the best of times, so leaving a trail of bitten and complaining creatures behind him suited Wasp just fine.

As night approached, the two servants of Khan-Garid met in front of the great eagle's palace. Swallow was beginning to worry that she would be punished for singing the day away. So she hoped that Wasp had found the tastiest animal in the world.

"Friend Wasp," she said, "did you find the tastiest animal in the world?"

"I did indeed," cried the eager Wasp. "After tasting the blood of hundreds of creatures I've determined that humans are the tastiest of all! I shall tell the great Khan that he should only enjoy the delicious meat of the humans at all his meals."

Hearing this, Swallow fell silent. She was shocked to hear Wasp's report. She liked the men, women, and children who often listened to her songs, cheered at her flying abilities, and left seeds and fruit as her reward. How could she save these friends from the cruel fate that awaited them if Wasp told Khan his findings?

Finally, Swallow had an idea. "How did you manage to taste the blood of so many creatures?" she asked.

"That was easy," said Wasp. "I just pierced them with my stinger and tasted their blood with my tongue."

"What an amazing feat," said Swallow. "How fortunate you are to be able to sense the most delicate of flavors. May I see this wonderful tongue of yours?"

Flattery often works wonders. When Wasp opened his mouth to show his tongue, Swallow bent down quickly, caught the tiny tongue in her beak, and snipped it off. Wasp flew backward in shock, but before he could say a word, the two servants were called in to see the great Khan.

Khan-Garid was eager to hear what they had found out, and he said, "Wasp, you tell me first whose meat tastes the best."

Wasp buzzed and buzzed but, without a tongue, he could not speak. He flew around the Khan's head and tried to tell him, but all that came out of his mouth was a loud and meaningless sound.

"What are you saying, Wasp? I can't understand a word. Leave me alone. Get out." The Khan took his majestic wing and shooed the Wasp from his face.

"Swallow, you tell me who has the tastiest meat."

"Well, my Khan, I have found on my journey that the snake has the tastiest meat in all the world."

Satisfied and ready for a grand meal, the Khan thanked the Swallow and told his court that from then on he would hunt the snake. And so it is that even today the eagle, the descendant of Khan-Garid, still hunts snakes and carries them to the nest to feed its young.

As for Swallow, she still soars through the sky and sings her songs to the delight of all creatures, including humans. Wasp, on the other hand, will buzz around your head trying to make you understand him until, finally in utter frustration, he stings you.

Notes

There are more than 100,000 species of wasps throughout the world. The Asian giant hornet is the largest with a wingspan of three inches and a body that is two inches long. Wasps are only active during the day. Swallows are found all over the world and are characterized by their acrobatic flying and their ability to feed while flying. They make their nests in hollow trees, or burrow in sand banks or make their nests of mud. Their main food source is insects but oddly enough they avoid stinging insects like wasps.

—DK

The Birds' Garden

A folktale from Kazakhstan

Once there were two neighbors, a shepherd whose land was rocky and poor but perfect for his sheep and a farmer whose land was rich and grew wonderful fruits and vegetables. Over the years these men and their families became good friends—their children played together, their wives cooked together, the men helped each other in their work, and the families went to the mosque together.

One summer a terrible disease swept through the herds of the shepherd and killed all of the sheep. Soon after, the shepherd packed his family and started a long journey to the city. As they were leaving, they were stopped by the farmer, who asked "where are you going?"

"Without my sheep, we cannot stay here. Perhaps we can beg for food in the city," replied the shepherd.

The farmer thought for a moment and said, "I will give you half my land. My farm can easily be divided. Each of us will have enough to feed our family and prosper."

"No," said the shepherd. "It isn't right for you to sacrifice for us."

"Of course it is right," laughed the farmer. "Good friends and neighbors are hard to come by."

And so, it was decided to divide the farm, and the shepherd was given half. He and his family worked hard on their new farm, and the farmer next door was happy that his dear friends were still his neighbors.

One day, the shepherd and his son were clearing some land that was covered by thick hedges. As they dug up the roots of one bush, they struck

Maui and the Birds

A folktale from the Maori people of New Zealand

Maui noticed that the sun moved too quickly as it traveled across the sky. People had barely started to fish or work in the garden or cook and it was already dark. "If my brothers and I bind the sun with ropes," he thought, "this will slow his progress across the heavens." At first his brothers argued that Maui's idea was all foolishness, but Maui soon convinced them to try. They plaited strong ropes and took them to the cave where the sun emerged every day. The first time they caught the sun he merely burned up their ropes. The second time Maui made the ropes from green flax. When he caught the sun, the ropes held tight. Then Maui took his magical weapon, the jawbone of Muri-ranga-whenua, and beat the sun until he promised to slow his progress across the sky and give people more daylight.

After his battle with the sun, Maui was scorched and dry but he saw no water to quench his thirst. He did see some birds nearby and called out to them.

From the time that Maui was a boy he had a special bond with birds. He knew all their names and their customs, where they liked to perch, and what they liked to eat. Whenever he spoke to them, they seemed to understand what he was saying. In fact, Maui could also change himself into a bird when he wanted to play a trick on someone or if he needed to escape danger.

Maui looked up and saw a saddleback bird. "Please, my friend," he called, "can you bring me some water. I am so thirsty and so hot."

But the thoughtless saddleback bird refused. So Maui grabbed it, squeezed it tight, and then threw it away. The place where he touched it still bears the mark of Maui's hand.

Then Maui saw the stitchbird and called out to him. "My friend can you bring me some water to quench this terrible thirst of mine. The sun is so hot; it is baking me."

But the foolish stitchbird also refused to bring Maui water, so he caught it and threw it into the flames of the sun and ever since the bird has a breast as yellow as fire itself.

The third bird that Maui was saw a robin, a bird that had always been his favorite. "My old friend, can you help me by bringing me some water," he cried. "I am so hot and the sun is just baking me alive."

The robin loved Maui and called back, "I will bring you water but I am so small it will only be a drop or two. I hope that will be enough."

The robin flew close to Maui and placed a drop or two of water into his mouth.

Maui thanked the robin and, to show his gratitude, he turned the feathers at the front of robin's head snowy white.

Since he was still thirsty, Maui then called out to the orange-wattled crow. "Crow my old friend, can you bring me some water to help me on this hot day?"

The crow dove into the water and filled his mouth and his ears with water and brought it to Maui. Maui was so grateful that he made the legs of the crow longer and more slender so he could move through the water faster in search of food.

And from that time until today, Maui has never forgotten the kindness of the crow and robin.

Notes

In the mythology of the Polynesian people, Maui is their cultural hero. He performs great deeds and his legends are spread across the Pacific from New Zealand to Hawaii. The Polynesians arrived in New Zealand around 1250 C.E. and developed the distinct Maori culture. The island nation of New Zealand is located 900 miles east of Australia.

—DK

Marko Kraljevic and the Eagle

A folktale from Serbia

Marko Kraljevic staggered along the road. The great hero of Serbia and the Balkans was ill and shook with fever. He stabbed his spear into the ground and tethered his warhorse, Sharatz, to the shaft. Marko slumped to the ground and leaned his back against the spear.

He wrapped his great green cloak around him and fell into a fitful sleep. He could not keep his eyes open, but when he slept, he could only see the horrors of all the battles he had fought and all the suffering he had seen. Suddenly a huge gray eagle landed on the top of the spear. The eagle spread her wings and made shade for the feverish warrior and several times a day she poured cold water on him from her beak. Day after day the eagle stood guard over the warrior and protected him.

As Marko returned to health, he looked up at the eagle and asked, "Why are you here, my friend? What have I ever done for you to deserve such kindness?"

The eagle looked down at Marko with the sharp eyes of a hunter and said, "Do not be foolish, Marko. At the Battle of Kosovo, a stray arrow found its mark in my body. The enemy would have cut my wings from my body if you hadn't saved me. You set me high in a fir tree out of the danger of the battle. After the battle, you gave me food to eat and water to drink and took me to the mountains where you united me with my little ones. You held them in your arms and kept them warm and found a safe place for me to raise my young."

"Ah, I remember that now," replied Marko, as visions of that great battle and the wounded eagle flooded his memory.

"After all you did for me, you ask why I do these little things for you? Some men may call you enemy, but I will always call you hero and friend."

And so it was.

Notes

In the animal world, the eagle has some of the best vision. Some studies report an eagle being able to spot an animal the size of a rabbit from up to two miles away. Eagles mate for life and the female eagle is larger than the male. The nest of an eagle is called an eyrie. The white-tailed eagle has an impressive 7-foot plus wingspan but that's not even close to the bird with the biggest wingspan—the wandering albatross whose wingspan measures over 12 feet across.

—DK

The Man, the Dove, and the Hawk

A folktale from Nigeria

Once there was a man who was both blind and lame. One evening he sat beneath the trees that stood in front of his house, lamenting that he could not see the wonders around him nor run and feel the wind in his face.

Without warning a dove flew down and hid beneath his robes. Within seconds a hawk swooped down and landed on a low branch just above his head. The hawk begged the man to give him the dove. "I have not eaten in days and days," he said. "By giving me the dove to feast upon you will be saving my life. If you give me the dove, then I will give you your sight in return."

Hearing this, the dove also pleaded with the man. "If you do what the hawk asks, you will be releasing me to my death. If you save me, I promise to cure your lameness. You will be able to walk again."

The blind man was perplexed. Who should he help? The hawk? The dove? Both promised him a reward but the man was unsure who he should save and who he should condemn to death. He sent for a friend whose advice he trusted. "Should I regain my sight or the use of my legs?" he asked.

The friend did not know what to say to the unfortunate man. Sadly, he shook his head and answered, "You'll have to paddle your own boat. I cannot help you decide." The friend left the man there to make his own decision.

The man thought for a while and finally said to the hawk, "What would you think if I gave you a chicken instead of the dove?"

The hawk was over joyed. "I'd much rather have a chicken than a dove. If you give me a chicken, I will leave now and never bother you or the dove again."

The man replied, "Since I am providing you with food, you must keep your promise and help cure my blindness." Then he said to the dove, "Since I am saving your life, you must keep your promise and help me regain the use of my legs."

Both birds agreed.

The hawk told the man he must pick the leaves of a certain plant, prepare them, and squeeze the juice into his eyes. "When you do this, your sight will be restored," said the hawk as he flew off with his chicken.

Next the dove told the man what to do to regain the use of his legs. Then the man released the dove who flew high into the trees.

The grateful man followed the instructions given by both birds and regained his sight and the use of his legs.

Notes

Nigeria, also called the Federal Republic of Nigeria, lies on the west coast of Africa. It is the most populous country in Africa and is home to over 500 different ethnic groups.

—DK

Crane Child

A folktale from Japan

L ong ago, in a distant land, there lived a poor old man and his wife. Gathering wood from the neighboring mountain forest, they worked hard breaking it into kindling to sell in the village below. They were never blessed with children to help them in their elder years, but they were happy in each other's company.

Once a week the old man made a trip down to the village to sell the bundle of sticks. One afternoon the snowflakes danced and dusted the path as the old man started down the worn path to the village with his load of sticks. Suddenly, he heard a strange cry and a shuffling sound. He hurried toward the noise and discovered a crane, the color of a lustrous pearl, caught in a snare. The look of terror and fear in the eyes of this magnificent creature stirred the old man. He spoke in a soft voice as one would to a frightened child. Slowly, he edged toward the crane who gradually stopped flapping its wings and watched the old man. He reached the rope and untangled the crane's leg. Spreading its wide wings, the crane swiftly flew up into the snowflakes.

An angry voice shouted, "That was MY bird you released."

The old man turned around to see a large red-faced man pounding toward him.

"I am sorry," the old man said. "Please, take my kindling wood in payment."

The man grunted, but took the offered bundle and left. Empty-handed, the old man returned home whistling a happy tune along the way. He did not notice the crane who circled three times above him before flying away. At home, the old man told his wife the story of the crane.

She smiled, "You did the right thing, my dear. We have enough money to last until next week. But to make up for our loss, next time I will also carry a load of wood with you to the village. I am glad you are safely at home. The snowstorm has gotten worse and you might have frozen."

The wife was preparing soup and rice for supper when they heard a knock on the door. A girl dressed in a thin white kimono stood shivering at their door. The couple looked at each other in surprise.

"I have lost my way," she said in a small voice, unused to speaking. "May I spend the night?"

They brought her to the fire to warm herself and the wife said, "We do not have much but you are welcome to stay as long as you need."

She prepared a bed for the child who ate some rice and then fell asleep, exhausted. The next morning, the couple awoke to the smell of breakfast cooking. The girl had swept the room and made the morning meal.

"Obaa-san (Grandmother), Ojii-san (Grandfather) please come and have breakfast," the girl said.

The old woman smiled, "You are the daughter we always wanted. Please stay with us as long as you like."

The girl made life very pleasant by helping with chores. One day she said, "I would like to weave something for you to sell in the village. Do you have any threads?"

The old woman showed the girl to the loom and the old man bought weaving yarns for her. The girl placed a large screen around the loom and said, "I will weave for you, but you must not look at me at any time while I am weaving. This you must promise."

The old man and woman promised they would leave her undisturbed. Hidden behind the screen, the girl began to weave. The old couple heard the whoosh of shuttle slide and the clacking sound of the loom. The girl worked without rest for three days. The old woman called to her to offer food, but the girl refused. At the end of the third day, the sounds of weaving stopped and the girl presented the old man with a bolt of elegant brocade.

"Go to the village to sell this, but do not quote a price," she said.

The old man went to the village and offered the brocade. Merchants came to look and they began to bid for the lovely fabric. Finally, a rich man offered a 100 pieces of gold for it! It was more money than the old man ever imagined. The old man smiled as he bought good things to eat and gifts for his family. The gold would last them for a long while.

A week later, the girl said to the old couple, "I will weave another cloth for you but remember, do not try to look upon me while I am weaving."

They readily agreed. The girl returned to the loom sheltered behind the screen where the sounds of weaving once again filled the little home. The old man wondered about her secret. The old woman wished to learn the girl's wonderful weaving technique. They thought a little peek wouldn't hurt as long as they did not disturb her.

Quietly, they approached the screen and through the thin gap between the wall and the screen they viewed a pearly-white crane at the loom. She was plucking the downy feathers from her breast to weave into the luminescent cloth. The old woman gasped, but the crane kept weaving.

The crane wove until early the next morning; then as a girl, she emerged from behind the screen with her arms weighed down with a bolt of fabric that seemed to glow. She handed the fabric to the old man.

"I have made this for you, Ojii-san, in payment for saving my life. Since you discovered the secret of who I really am, I must go now."

"We are sorry," the old man pleaded. "Please do not leave us. We love you like our own daughter."

The girl opened the door and walked outside. The couple looked at each other in despair and then followed the girl outside. But she was gone. Seeing tracks in the snow, they bent down and discovered the footprints of a crane. They heard a cry above them and watched the crane circle three times overhead before disappearing forever into the misty gray clouds surrounding the mountain.

Notes

Cranes make their homes in wetland areas, shallow lakes, or slow moving rivers. They are found all over the world except South America and Antarctica. With long necks and legs, these large birds range in length from 35 inches (90 cm) to 69 inches (176 cm). They live up to 25 years and mate for life. Omnivorous eaters, cranes feed on anything including fish, amphibians, small rodents, berries, and grains depending upon the season and availability of food. Their numbers are declining as their habitats are destroyed.

In Japan, the crane has special significance. It symbolizes happiness, longevity, and good fortune. After World War II, the crane came to signify peace, healing, and hope. Inspired by an ancient senbazuru legend, a girl named Sadako began to make origami cranes with the goal of creating 1,000 cranes to gain a wish. Sadako suffered from leukemia, most likely caused by radiation from the atomic bomb dropped on Hiroshima. In 1955, she died of her illness and in commemoration of her, there is a statue of her holding a crane at Hiroshima Peace Park. Every year, people leave paper cranes at the statue in memory of their ancestors and with a wish for happiness.

—KB

The Pheasants and the Bell

A folktale from Korea

Once a long time ago there lived a woodcutter. One day he went deep into the woods to gather firewood to sell in the village. As he walked along, he heard the sound of pheasants. As he came closer to the sound, he saw the birds flying up and down in a panic. Then he saw a huge snake threatening the eggs in their nest. The woodcutter took his stout walking stick and tried to move the snake away but it kept coming back to the pheasants' nest. Finally he struck the snake, hoping to stun it and carry it away from the nest, but the woodcutter's blow was so powerful the snake died. The pheasants landed in their nest and soon quieted down. While the woodcutter was sad that he had killed the snake, at least he knew that he had saved the eggs and they would grow to be beautiful birds.

Many years later the woodcutter was on a long journey and lost his way during a terrible storm. The woods seemed to close around him as the storm raged in the sky and rain pelted down on him. Then he saw a light ahead and walked quickly toward it. As he approached, he saw a small hut under an overhang of a cliff, and standing in the doorway was a young woman who beckoned him to come out of the storm into her home. The hut was neat with a welcoming fire glowing in the center.

"Do you live here alone?" asked the woodcutter.

"Yes, I am all alone," she replied.

"It seems to be a lonely life so deep in the woods and so far from any village," he remarked.

"It was until now," she said. Then she began to change. The air shimmered and snapped and she changed from a beautiful young woman into an enormous snake. "But now you are here my enemy and my time here is fulfilled."

The woodcutter was shocked. "Why am I your enemy?"

"Years ago you killed me in the woods and now I am going to kill you slowly and painfully." The ghostly snake started to move toward the woodcutter.

The man remembered the incident and said, "I was protecting those eggs. I had no intention of killing you. I just wanted to get you away from the nest. It was an accident."

"Accident or not I have floated in these woods as a ghost waiting on my chance for revenge and I will not be denied." The snake seemed to smile as it crawled closer.

"Wait," the man pleaded, "please give me a chance to redeem myself."

The snake stopped and seemed to think about the man's request. "There is a ruined temple about a quarter a mile from here. In the old tower there hangs a bell. If you can make the bell ring from here, then it will be a sign that the gods want me to spare your life. Try and make the bell ring out."

The woodcutter knew that it was impossible. "I cannot make the bell ring from here."

The snake started to move toward him again. "Then I must kill you."

Suddenly they both heard the sound of a bell ring through the storm and then another peal sounded out.

The snake stopped and said, "It is the wish of the gods that I will not have my revenge. I will leave this earth and never bother you again my enemy." With those words the snake disappeared and then the fire and the hut, leaving the woodcutter under the overhang of the small cliff. The storm stopped and the night was silent.

The man fell to the ground exhausted and slept in the shelter of the cliff. In the morning he woke and walked to the ruins of the abandoned temple. He approached the tower that housed the bell and fell to his knees. There on the bell were two spots of blood and on the ground were the broken bodies of two pheasants that had flown into the bell to make it ring. They had repaid his kindness by sacrificing their lives to save him.

Notes

The Chinese consider the Golden Pheasant a sign of good luck and prosperity. Pheasants have an uncanny awareness of their surroundings and can detect danger quickly. The natural habitat of the pheasant is grasslands near water with groups of trees close by. The ability of the pheasant to adapt to many environments and climates has spread it to many countries making it one of the most hunted birds in the world.

—DK

The Waiting Maid and the Parrot

A folktale from China

A long time ago there was a beautiful young woman who served as a waiting maid in a great household. The master of the house was so impressed by her beauty and intelligence that he gave her the task of caring for a parrot that had been given to his family by a powerful government official.

One day she was alone with the bird when it began to speak to her. "Take care of me well young lady and you will be rewarded with a good husband."

The girl was so startled that she reached out and swatted the parrot with her fan. The bird started talking to her regularly and soon she was responding. She and the parrot were alone together so much that they soon became friends, and she took the parrot into her confidence about her hopes and dreams.

One day as she was bathing, the bird left its cage and started to fly around the room. She often left the cage open but the parrot had always stayed close to her. She tried to stop the bird but she flew into the garden and over the wall. The girl was so terrified that she would be punished for losing the prize pet that she moved the cage out onto the veranda. She told the master that while she was bathing someone had come along and let the bird out. The master knew that many of the other maids were jealous of her and envied her light workload so he believed her story.

A few days later she was sent on an errand to the house of a widow. As she approached the house, a parrot flew into the room of the woman's son Liang Hsu and spoke to him. "I have decided to help you find the perfect woman to marry. You should go out and see her." Liang Hsu followed the bird to the courtyard and saw the waiting maid. Her beauty captured his heart at once. He followed her to his mother's room and listened as they spoke and learned she was as intelligent as she was lovely. He heard that she worked in the household of a great house. Once in a while she would glance his way, and each time their eyes met, they each knew that they liked the other. When the young man returned to his room, he realized that the parrot had disappeared.

The waiting maid returned to her master's household thinking of the handsome young man who had silently watched her. When she entered her room, she saw the parrot on top of the cage, eyes closed. She rushed to capture her but she fluttered away and scolded her. "Now haven't I been busy all day trying to find a proper husband for you and now you try and throw me back into that cage? Listen and I'll tell you what I've been up to today."

The girl listened as the parrot told her what she had done that afternoon. "I cannot carry you away on my wings but I can be your way to communicate with each other." The bird thought she heard someone coming and quickly flew out the window.

The girl sat on her bed and thought about what had happened to her that day. She knew that the parrot was looking out for her but she also knew that the young man would never want a girl that served in another household.

The next day the bird appeared again and the girl spoke, "I thank you for all you have done for me but the master dotes on me and will never let me go to another household to wed. Besides, Liang Hsu may not want to marry someone of my low rank. Thank you for your help but it is hopeless." The bird stretched her wings and flew away without a word.

The parrot returned after dark and recited a poem that Liang Hsu had composed for her. When the girl heard his words of love and devotion, she had the parrot recite the short poem over and over again.

At dawn the parrot flew straight to Liang Hsu's home and told him of the girl's response. Liang Hsu wrote out a letter asking her to marry him. The parrot grabbed the letter in her beak and took it to the young woman. The parrot read the letter to her since her tears of joy filled her eyes and she could not read it. She told the parrot to tell Liang Hsu to go to her parents and make propose a dowry of marriage. Then she could be free of her master's household. She gave the parrot one of her earrings as a token to give to Liang Hsu.

As the parrot flew to Liang Hsu's house, a young boy threw a rock at it and it fell dead to the ground. Now the two young people had no way to talk to each other. But that was not the only disaster that entered their life. The other servants did not like the idea that the serving girl was a favorite with their master so they hatched a plot to get rid of her. They accused her of seeing another man and stole Liang Hsu's letter as proof. The master was so angry that he struck the girl and she fell unconscious to the ground. Trying to hide his crime, he had her buried in a shallow grave outside of the town.

That night Liang Hsu had a dream. A woman came to him dressed in white feathers from her neck to her feet. She told the young man that she was the sister of the waiting maid and that they had both been parrots in another life. "My sister was so good that she was reborn a human, a beautiful girl. I was still a parrot. When I finally found her, I tried to find her a husband that was worthy of her kindness and beauty. I found you. Now, she has been falsely accused and buried alive by her cruel master. There is not much time but only you can bring her back to this world and heal her. She is buried one hundred paces from the city but hurry there is not much time." Then the woman fell to the ground and rose up and turned into a white crane and soared up into the heavens.

Liang Hsu woke up and took a servant with him to search for the grave. He remembered that there was a village outside the city called "One Hundred Paces" so he went there and near an abandoned temple he found the grave. He and his servant dug down and opened the coffin. She was barely alive, but when he kissed her, she opened her eyes and smiled. He carried her to a nearby convent where the nuns agreed to take care of her.

A month later the girl was healthy. He told his mother everything, and because she trusted her son, she agreed to meet the girl and accept her as her daughter-in-law. She went to the convent and talked to the girl and knew that she was as honest and kind as she was beautiful. She brought her home and she and Liang Hsu were married. They kept the fact she was alive a secret from her old master.

Liang Hsu remembered the kindness of the talking parrot, and every time that he saw someone selling a parrot in a cage in the market, he bought the bird and set it free and smiled as it soared through the sky.

Notes

There are 372 different species of parrots. They can live up to 80 years and are found in tropical and subtropical climates throughout the world. They are considered one of the smartest birds and studies show that the African gray parrot can understand the meaning of words and even form simple sentences.

—DK

The Rooster and the Sultan

A folktale from Hungary

Once, a long time ago, there was a poor old woman who lived all alone. She had no land, no money, and not a lot to eat. Though her neighbors tried to help her, they were almost as poor as she was and had little to share. All the old woman owned was a rooster who spent most of his days scrounging around the village dump.

One day, as the rooster was scratching around, it found a diamond penny. The rooster crowed and squawked, "Look what I found! Cock-a-doodle-doo. I found a diamond penny. Cock-a-doodle-doo. I found a diamond penny."

Just as he was crowing about his find, the Sultan was riding by with his guards. When he heard the rooster bragging about his discovery, he had to have the penny for himself. The Sultan was well known for his love of anything beautiful or precious.

"Rooster," cried the Sultan, "bring that penny to me immediately."

"Never," replied the rooster. "I am giving this diamond penny to my mistress."

The greedy ruler always got what he wanted so his guards took the penny away from the rooster. The Sultan placed the penny in the palace treasury.

The rooster was furious. He followed the Sultan, perched on top of the huge wall that surrounded the palace, crowing over and over again, "Give me back my diamond penny. The Sultan has stolen my diamond penny."

The Sultan had his servants lock all the windows and doors so he could not hear the rooster. This only made the rooster angrier. He flew against the windows, scratched with his feet and beak, screeching, "Give me back my diamond penny. The Sultan has stolen my diamond penny."

The Sultan turned to his Grand Vizier telling him to throw him down the well and drown him.

The Vizier threw the rooster into the well but that was not the end of the rooster. The rooster called to the water, "Water, water, pour into my belly." Every drop of water in the well poured into the rooster's belly and he flew out of the well. Once again he flew against the windows and scratched with his feet and beak, screeching, "Give me back my diamond penny. The Sultan has stolen my diamond penny."

The Sultan told the cook to catch the rooster and throw him into the oven. The cook did just that, but that was not the end of the rooster. He just called out, "Water, water, flow out of my belly." All the water he had swallowed in the well came gushing out and put out the fire, cooling the oven down. Once again the angry bird flew against the windows and scratched with his feet and beak, screeching, "Give me back my diamond penny. The Sultan has stolen my diamond penny."

Then Sultan had one of his guards shut the rooster up in a beehive. But that was not the end of the rooster. He called out, "Little bees, little bees, come hide under my wings." The bees hid under his wings and the rooster flew out of the beehive unharmed. Once again he flew against the windows and scratched with his feet and beak, screeching, "Give me back my diamond penny. The Sultan has stolen my diamond penny."

The Sultan was so angry he could not control himself. "Bring me that horrible rooster and I will sit on it and squash it to death."

The rooster was brought to the Sultan's throne room, but before the Sultan could sit on the rooster, the bird called out, "Little bees, little bees, come out from under my wings and sting the Sultan." The bees swarmed all around the Sultan and stung, and stung, and stung him.

"I am beaten," cried the miserable Sultan. "Go to my treasury and take your diamond penny and leave me in peace."

The rooster flew to the treasury and there was the diamond penny sitting on top of a pile of gold and jewels. The rooster called out, "Belly, belly, swallow every coin here that the Sultan has stolen." At those words every coin in the treasury flew into the belly of the rooster. Not one coin was left in the room.

Back in the village, the rooster spat every last gold coin and a huge pile of money filled the village square. His mistress shared all the money with the people of the village and they all lived in peace and prosperity forever.

Notes

Roosters are male chickens, while hens are female. Roosters crow early in the morning at a fixed time every day. They are larger, with longer tails and more brightly colored than the hens. Roosters are highly territorial and can be aggressive if they feel that they or their hens are in danger. Chickens are the most populous birds in the world—over 50 billion are raised every year for eggs and meat. Chickens were probably domesticated over 10,000 years ago. In many cultures the rooster is considered a magical bird.

—DK

Yogodayu and the Army of Bees

A *folktale from Japan*

In ancient Japan there once lived a great samurai named Yogodayu. He had been a hero in many battles, fighting for his emperor. When peace finally came to Japan, Yogodayu was happy to return with his warriors to the tranquility of his castle in Yamoto. However, war seemed to follow him home. His brother-in-law, a spiteful neighbor and ruthless warlord, wanted to possess all the lands near his castle, including those belonging to Yogodayu.

Suddenly, he attacked without any warning. Envious of Yogodayu, his land, and all of the attention he had got from the Emperor, he defeated the great samurai whose men fought bravely but were outnumbered. Yogodayu and his warriors were driven from their castle and fled for their lives into the mountains. There they found a huge complex of caves that were connected, an ideal place to hide and think of a strategy to overcome their enemy.

One day, as Yogodayu was walking through the valley below the caves, he came across a spider's web. Looking closely, he saw a huge bee that was caught in the web struggling for its life. Gently, the samurai freed the bee from the web, saying "Go back to your hive little warrior. I am honored to free something that has been trapped. I only wish I could do the same for myself and my men."

That night, as Yogodayu lay sleeping, he dreamed that a strange samurai dressed in black and yellow armor visited him.

"Sir," said the warrior, "I wish to help you as you helped me."

"Who are you and why do you want to help me?"

"I am the bee that you freed from the spider's web. I want to repay my debt to you. I have a plan that can help you defeat your enemy and regain your lands and castle."

"How can I defeat an enemy that outnumbers me and has already defeated my army?"

"With my help, you can. First, gather as many stragglers from your army and any others that will join your cause. Have each warrior bring jars and containers with them. Then build a wooden house at the end of the valley. Send word out that you are assembling an army to attack your brother-in-law. I will arrange everything else, and I promise you victory."

When Yogodayu woke up, he knew that what had happened in the dream was true. He sent trusted men out to gather others to his cause. As soon as more samurai arrived, he had them build a wooden house at the end of the valley and fill it with containers and jars. Soon they heard a loud and almost deafening buzzing sound. Then, a gigantic cloud of bees appeared, one so huge that it blocked out the sun. The bees flew into the house and into the jars. The sound of their buzzing grew quiet.

Quickly, Yogodayu sent out spies to spread the word that he was assembling a huge army to retake his land.

When his brother-in-law heard the news, he decided to attack before Yogodayu's army could become too big. When the spiteful warlord appeared in the valley, his men marched straight toward the wooden house. Yogodayu's small force then attacked. At first the force of their courage drove the enemy back, but soon the larger army gained force. Although Yogodayu's men fought bravely, it was clear that they could not defeat their enemy without help. Suddenly, the air was filled with the buzzing sound of thousands and thousands of bees. They flew out of the wooden house and began to sting the enemy warriors. They stung their faces, their necks, and their hands. They even stung them deep inside their armor. Soon the enemy was in complete retreat with Yogodayu's men and the bees striking them down from behind. The enemy army was broken and surrendered.

Yogodayu's army stormed their castle and took it back. With the battle over, then Yogodayu moved to bury the dead. He placed the fallen bees beside his fallen samurai and erected two temples—one to his loyal men and the other to the bees that had fought so bravely to help him regain his lands. He never forgot them, nor did his people.

———————————

Notes

Bees are the only insects that produce food (honey) that is eaten by people. The wings of a honeybee beat 200 times per second producing the buzzing sounds we associate with bees. Bees die after they sting.

—DK

Section 3

Creatures of the Water

The Samurai and the Sea Turtle

A folktale from Japan

Once a long time ago there lived a samurai named Fujiwara no Yamakage. When he was a young man, he went on a pilgrimage to Sumiyoshi. As he walked along the shore, a fisherman hailed him.

"Young sir, would you like to buy some fish? I have some beautiful fresh fish I caught this morning."

Politely, the young warrior looked into the boat. Instead of seeing the fish, the samurai's eyes were held by the steady gaze of a huge sea turtle—its fins were pinned together by spikes and its beak wrapped shut with rope. The eyes were dark and seemed to look deep into the young man.

"How much for the turtle?" asked the samurai.

"The turtle," exclaimed the fisherman. "He is worth a lot of money. The meat and the shell will fetch me a good price in the market."

Yamakage took off his expensive silk cloak and handed it to the fisherman. "Is this enough?"

The fisherman was delighted with the trade and helped the young man carry the turtle to the beach. There Yamakage carefully pulled the spikes from the turtle's fins. He washed the wounds and applied oinment that his mother had packed for him for his journey. He unwrapped the rope from its beak and brought fresh seawater for the turtle to drink and seaweed for the beast to eat. Then the samurai slept all night on the beach close to the sea turtle, protecting him. While the young man lay sleeping, the huge turtle gazed at him with wonder and affection, and dreamed of the sea. The next day, late in the afternoon, the turtle lumbered toward the sea and, with a final gaze at Yamakage and a flip of a fin, he slipped beneath the waves.

That night, as the samurai slept, the sea turtle came to him in a dream and spoke. "Thank you, young sir, for your kindness—you have truly saved my life. Always remember that when you need me I will be there for you." The young man woke refreshed and calm, as if he knew that a great friend was walking by his side, watching his every move.

The years passed by and Yamakage became a great lord, trusted by the shogun who ruled all of Japan. Now a great samurai, he married and had a son, but his wife died in childbirth, leaving him to care for the infant. Now a young child is not easy to care for, but the boy was the light of his father's heart. In time Yamakage decided to marry again. His new wife also seemed to love his son, telling him stories, singing him songs, and playing with him whenever Yamakage was near. It pleased him that she was so attached to his son. Appearances, however, can be deceiving.

In time Yamakage was made viceroy of Kyushu and set sail in a small convoy of ships for his new post. Being an important official, he sailed with his warriors and advisors, while his family and household sailed in another ship.

As the two ships sailed up the coast, they soon found themselves in a great storm. The winds lashed at the sails, and the seas pounded against the hulls. Suddenly, Yamakage heard cries from the other ship—his son had fallen overboard. His warriors, risking their very lives, searched the sea all night but they found no trace of the child.

When the first light of dawn played on the water, someone shouted that something was moving toward the ship. Yamakage watched in wonder as a dark shape came closer and closer—soon they made out that it was a child—it was his son. They realized that he was riding on the back of an enormous sea turtle. A shout of joy came from all the samurai as the boy neared his father's ship. He was lifted off the great turtle's back and handed to his father who held him tightly. Then Yamakage looked down at the turtle and saw scars where the spikes had pierced its fins. The samurai knew that this turtle was the one he had saved so many years ago.

The turtle stared up at him, as if he wanted to speak. Yamakage bent down and looked deep into those eyes, and once again he heard the turtle's voice in his head.

"My friend, I have come to fulfill my vow and bring your son back to you. Last night I saw the young master's stepmother throw him over the side of the ship. There was hate in her eyes and evil on her face. I caught him on

my back and kept him safe through the storm so that I could bring him back to one who truly loves him. Beware of that woman, for she has no love in her heart for you or your son." With those words the giant sea turtle swept its fins into the deep water and disappeared. Yamakage watched as if in a dream.

The great samurai returned to Kyoto, and his son was given into the care of the monks at the great temple. The boy grew up to become a scholar and a wise man who advised emperors and shoguns alike. After the death of his father, he took care of his stepmother in her old age. How terrible and humble she must have felt to be cared for by the stepson she had once tried to kill. The boy had grown to be a man like his father, kind to all around him.

Notes

Sea turtles excrete sea water through their eyes giving the appearance that they are crying. They are incredible divers and reach depths of over 3,000 feet. They are great swimmers and can reach speeds of five miles per hour and travel over 8,000 miles when they migrate. Once male turtles go into the sea as small hatchlings, they never come back to land again. Female turtles come to shore to lay their eggs and bury them in the warm sand.

The word samurai means "one who serves." The samurai made up the warrior class of Japan.

—DK

Frog Princess

A *folktale from Croatia*

Once there was and once there was not, a king who was cruel and evil. His advisor was a wicked wizard. Now this king had three sons. The oldest was as cruel as his father. The middle son was even worse. But the youngest son, Vinko, was kind and didn't have a mean bone in his body. The youngest son watched all the evil deeds his brothers committed and tried to fix them. If the oldest ripped up the royal garden, the youngest would plant all the flowers back and water them tenderly. If the middle brother kicked the royal hound, the youngest would pet the dog and give him a bone. The youngest was so good that all the people in the kingdom knew he would make the best king. They also knew that it would never happen.

Now the king was having money problems as kings usually have. He called his wizard to his side and asked him what could be done to find more money to pay for his royal excess. The wizard thought and finally spoke.

"Your majesty, we are in a dilemma. You see the normal ways of gaining money really are closed to us. We can't go to war and conquer your enemies because they've all beaten us in battle. We can't raise taxes because the people already pay 100% in taxes. But I do have an idea. We could marry the princes off to three wealthy families. Then we would have their money."

The king liked this idea. "But," he asked, "how can we be sure that the families will be rich?"

"We'll have a proclamation made that you are choosing wives for the boys. We'll go to the square and you will toss your crown into the air. Wherever it lands, the girl who lives there will be a bride. I'll use magic to make sure that they are wealthy and available."

And so the proclamation was made and the day came when the king, his wizard, and the three princes appeared in the square.

The king threw his crown into the air where it swirled and whirled and twirled until, as if by magic, it fell on the roof of the richest merchant in town. His daughter would marry the eldest prince.

The king threw his crown in the air a second time and it swirled and whirled and twirled until it fell, as if by magic, on the roof of the richest banker in town. Not only was he rich but he had plenty of other people's money too. His daughter would marry the second prince.

The king threw his crown one last time and it swirled and whirled and twirled but it didn't fall on any house, instead it flew over the city walls and landed in a lake.

The king looked at the wizard and said, "Get in the boat and row me out there."

They rowed out into the middle of the lake only to find that the crown didn't fall in the water after all but fell on a tiny, little island. When the king picked up the crown, there was a frog underneath and the frog spoke.

"Good afternoon, gracious king."

The king and the wizard were shocked.

"A talking frog?" said the king. "How can this be?"

The wizard had no answers at all. He merely looked at the frog with his mouth wide open.

"I've heard of your proclamation and I have a lovely daughter."

The king's mind turned to evil immediately. What a great way to get back at his all too sweet son and teach him a lesson.

"Bring her to me."

The frog dove into the lake and came back with a beautiful little frog all covered in red and green.

"Take good care of my baby."

"Oh I will," said the king. "I'll treat her like my own daughter."

When he got back to the shore, he walked straight to Vinko and held out his hand with the little frog in his palm and said, "Meet your new wife."

His brothers howled with laughter and so did their intended brides for they were as ill-tempered as the princes.

The next day there was a wedding. The first bride wore silk, the second satin, and the little frog had on a tiny white veil.

At the wedding dinner, the first princess sipped her soup daintily, the second princess ate her salad sweetly, and the little frog waited for a fly to buzz by and then slurp went her tongue and the fly was gone. At every meal the little frog would catch all the bugs that flew by her much to the disgust of her fellow princesses and to the growing delight of Vinko.

One day, the two princesses, who were fitting in quite nicely in their evil little way, went to the king and demanded that the frog princess be sent away and that too sweet husband of hers, Vinko, too. The king was delighted to have an excuse to get his youngest son out of his sight and he had to admit that the joke had worn thin, especially at mealtime. So he banished Vinko and his bride to a small hunting cottage at the edge of the woods far from the palace, the city, and the royal family.

But Vinko was happy with his new life and he hoped that his little frog princess was too. Each day, he would go off into the woods and hunt and pick wild berries and yams. Each day he was amazed when he returned that the house was neat as a pin, there was a pot of strong tea on the stove, and even the clothes were washed and neatly folded. Who could be doing all this work while he was gone? Surely, it was not the frog.

One day, he decided to solve the mystery. He called out to the frog that he would be back later and took his bow and left the cottage. Instead, he climbed a tree that looked into the cottage and hid among the branches. He hadn't waited long when the frog hopped into view. She looked out the door and gazed in every direction. Then she hopped into the middle of the room and slowly began to grow. Larger and larger until she was as tall as a woman and then she took her hands and slowly peeled the frog skin from off herself. When she finished, there stood a beautiful young woman. She was dressed in a gown of red and green, the same colors as the frog skin. She waltzed around the room and disappeared into the kitchen singing an old song. Vinko sat in the tree in amazement and knew he was in love with his frog princess.

The next day he hid himself in the tree again and after she had changed and danced into the next room, Vinko ran into the house and took the frog skin and threw it into the fire place. She ran in and shouted, "Oh, my prince, you have broken the spell put on me so long ago and now I will be as you see, your princess forever." They danced and laughed and rejoiced at their good fortune. But good fortune is like a good story, it is hard to keep to oneself. Word spread throughout the kingdom that Prince Vinko's frog princess was a lovely lady, as kind and as good as he. The people started to say out loud how grand it would be if they could be the next king and queen. These words eventually reached the ears of the king and he was not happy.

"We have to get rid of them. They are a threat to my throne."

"Well," said the wizard. "I'm sure we could find a way but we have to be careful. The people have always loved Vinko and his new bride makes him all the more popular. We must have a reason. I know. We'll give him three tasks to perform and if he fails his father, the king, then he and his frog princess will be executed or exiled."

"Good. Very good. But what can we come up with that will ensure failure?" asked the king.

"I have a few things in mind that will undoubtedly baffle him," the wizard replied.

The next day Prince Vinko was escorted into the king's throne room.

"Vinko," said his royal father. "There are a few tasks I want done; I want them done correctly and by you. If you fail, you and your bride will pay with your lives. The first is that I want you to find a pot filled with food that can feed the whole army and still be full after the meal. Go."

When Vinko returned home, he was close to tears and told his wife they were lost. When he explained what had to be done, she smiled. "My mother has a pot just like that at the bottom of the lake. Go ask her."

Vinko walked to the lake and called out, "mother-in-law, mother-in-law."

The frog swam to the surface and called out, "yes son what do you want?"

"Oh, mother-in-law, I need a pot that can feed the whole army and still be full after the meal. Can you help us?"

"No problem." She dove to the bottom of the lake and told him to return the pot when he was done.

That afternoon the whole army assembled. Each man was given a large portion from the pot and yet when the meal was over the pot was full. The king and the wizard could not believe their eyes.

The next day, Vinko was again given an impossible task.

"This afternoon I want you to bring me a blanket that can cover the entire army while they sleep. If you do not, you both die."

Vinko went home near tears again and told his wife what his father had asked of him. "What are we going to do?" he cried.

"My mother has a blanket like that at the bottom of the lake. Go ask her for her help."

Vinko went to the lake and called, "mother-in-law, mother-in-law."

The frog rose to the surface and said, "yes son, what do you want?"

"Mother-in-law, I need a blanket that can cover the entire army while they sleep. Can you help us?"

"No problem." She dove to the bottom of the lake and came up with a blanket. She told him to return it after he was finished.

Vinko went to the barracks and the blanket stretched across all five thousand men, even enough room for the regimental dog. The king was baffled and the wizard was mystified. Where could he be getting these magical things?

The next day the king and the wizard came up with a task no one could accomplish. Vinko was summoned to the palace.

"Vinko, I want you to take me and the wizard and your two brothers so high into the sky we can see the whole kingdom at one time. If you fail . . ." Vinko knew what he would say next.

He went back to his princess and told her the whole story. "We are doomed," he cried. "No one can help us."

His wife smiled. "Go to my mother. She always has an answer for every problem."

Vinko went to the lake and called out, "mother-in-law, mother-in-law."

From the depths of the lake the frog swam. "Yes son, what do you want?"

"Mother-in-law, I have to take my father and brothers and the wizard high enough to see the whole kingdom. If not, we are doomed. Can you help us?"

"No problem." The frog called over eight huge geese from the other side of the lake and whispered in their ears.

"Take my friends here with you. They will take care of everything."

The eight geese followed Vinko through the streets while all the citizens watched, fearful for his safety.

When they got to the palace gates, the king, his sons, and the wizard were waiting.

"Well, can you do what I asked?" cried the king. The wizard and the other princes smirked in satisfaction.

"I think my friends here can take care of it all."

Suddenly two geese leapt up and grabbed the king by the shoulders, two grabbed the wizard, and the others grabbed the princes. Higher and higher they flew until the whole kingdom was in plain view.

"It's beautiful," cried the king. "Now take me down."

The geese all replied, "quack, quack, quack."

"Take me down right now."

"Quack, quack, quack, quack, quack."

"I am the king now take me down."

"Quack, quack, quack, quack, quack, quack, quack."

The geese flew to a desert island and dropped the four of them. The king and his wizard and the two unpleasant princes were never seen again.

Vinko became the king, the frog princess his queen. They reigned in peace and harmony with justice and kindness. The mother-in-law came to live in the palace pond and did what all mothers-in-law do best—she gave everyone the best advice.

Notes

Frogs are amphibians and need to live near water. They have very strong back legs that can help them jump over twenty times their own length. The longest frog jump on record is thirty-three feet and five inches. Frogs can absorb both water and oxygen through their skins. They shed their skins often, and after they have shed the old skin, they eat it.

—DK

Arion and the Dolphin

A folktale from Ancient Greece

Arion was the greatest singer of his time. His fame had spread across Greece and far beyond. When he practiced his lyre and sang his songs, people in the street would stop to listen, losing all track of time as the songs wove their spells. He was invited to the court of King Periander of Corinth to entertain the king and his guests.

One day, word reached Arion of a singing competition that was being held in Sicily. At first, Periander was reluctant to let him go but eventually the singer convinced the king that winning the prize would bring even greater glory to Corinth. In Sicily, he won every event that he entered and was crowned the champion. Bearing a treasure for himself and King Periander, he would return to Corinth an honored man.

At the port of Tarentum, Arion hired a ship that was manned by Corinthian sailors and set sail with his riches. But luck was not with Arion that day. The men he hired were pirates who plotted to kill him and steal his riches. They knew of the great singer's fame, so they decided they would make up a story, telling everyone that Arion had sailed on a different ship and fallen overboard during a great storm and drowned.

When Arion overheard the pirates planning, he pleaded with them. He offered the crew all his riches in return for his life, but his words fell on deaf ears. They argued that he would tell the truth when they reached Corinth and have them arrested. He would have to die.

"If I must die," said Arion, "may I have one last request?"

"And what is it?" asked the leader of the pirates.

"May I play my harp and sing one last song?"

The men agreed and Arion sat down on the deck and began to sing the Orthian, a high, sad melody to the gods. Even his hard-hearted captors were enthralled by his singing and listened in awe as the melody washed over them. His voice floated across the water and its beauty caught the attention of a dolphin who swam up next to the ship to hear the song. As the music ebbed and flowed, the dolphin seemed to sway with the tune. She raised her head out of the water so she could hear every word of the lament as the young singer poured out his heart in one last song.

Then, when the song ended, the cruel crew seized Arion, threw him overboard, and sailed away leaving him in the empty sea. As the ship disappeared toward the horizon, the dolphin swam up beside the exhausted Arion and nuzzled him. She then dove down and rose to the surface with the singer on her back. As the dolphin and her passenger swam through the sea, Arion was sure that he could hear her singing his song sweetly and softly as the water washed over them. Some say the gods, hearing this, calmed the sea and the wind so their voyage home would be safe. After many days at sea the two reached the Greek mainland. The dolphin left Arion near the shore and, with a flourish of her tail and a leap toward the sky, was gone. Arion, overjoyed to be on land, journeyed back to Corinth and the court of the king to tell his story.

Sadly, Periander did not believe Arion's story. He thought that the young singer was surely trying to keep all the riches for himself. In anger, the king had Arion put under guard and ordered his men to find the sailors who could come to the court and tell the true story.

A few days later the pirates appeared at the court of Periander and told their tale. "We heard that the great singer Arion was on a boat to Corinth when a great storm swept him over board. The ship and all the treasure were lost at sea."

Arion then stepped from behind a curtain and confronted the men who could not believe their eyes and begged for their lives. They confessed their crime and the treasure was recovered. Periander had them punished and restored Arion to his rightful place at the court.

Arion had one more thing to do before his adventure was complete. He built a shrine with a statue of a dolphin carrying a man on her back through the sea. "All people who pass," he said, "must know the kindness of those that dwell in the sea."

Notes

Dolphins are found in both salt and fresh water. They range in size from four feet up to the orca (killer whale), which can reach lengths of thirty plus feet. Dolphins have been observed caring for injured, sick, or elderly members of their pods—the name for a group of dolphins. Dolphins love to play and can be seen tugging and tossing seaweed and teasing and chasing each other through the water. They also make contact with humans by swimming in front of boats—the boat pushes them through the water as it plows through the sea. There have been many instances of dolphins saving people from drowning and even from shark attacks.

—DK

The Golden Crab

A *folktale from Greece*

In a certain kingdom, in a certain land in a little village, there lived a fisherman and his wife. Every day, the fisherman would cast his nets to catch fish to sell to the king. One bright blue morning, he discovered a golden crab in his fishing nets. He was so taken by this unusual creature that he set the beautiful crab on a shelf and took the rest of his catch to the palace to sell.

His wife went about her chores preparing fish when the crab spoke to her. Startled, she dropped her fish-cleaning knife and listened to his request. When her husband returned, she placed the crab on a dish and put the dish on the supper table. As the couple began to eat, they heard the golden crab's squeaky voice cry out, "Please, give me something to eat."

The husband's mouth dropped open and his eyes grew wide. The wife nodded. On a plate, she broke bread into small pieces for the crab. When the meal was over, the fisherman came to fetch the crab's dinner plate only to find it was heaped with gold coins.

Each day, after a meal, the wife or the fisherman would find the crab's dinner plate full of gold coins. Over time, they enjoyed his company and grew fond of him.

One day the crab said to the fisherman's wife. "It is time that I marry. Please, go to the king and tell him that I wish to marry his youngest daughter."

The wife thought to say something to the crab about the king's reaction, but then thought better. Surely this golden crab is a magical creature and knows what he is about. So, she went to the king with the crab's proposal.

The king thought the woman was mad, but decided to put this crab to a test. Perhaps this was an enchanted prince in disguise.

"Tell the crab, I will give my daughter's hand in marriage," he said, "if he builds a wall in front of my castle that is higher than my highest tower and on top of the wall must bloom flowers from around the world."

To fulfill the king's request, the crab gave the wife a golden rod, thick as her thumb and long as her arm. He told her to strike the ground three times in front of the castle. The next morning, a wall stood in front of the castle, taller than the highest turret, and brimming at the top with red, yellow, purple, and blue flowers from around the world. When the fisherman's wife returned the king was staring up at the wall.

"The crab has done your bidding, your majesty, and wishes to marry your daughter," she said.

The king stroked his beard and said, "Tell the crab there is yet one more task he must complete to win the hand of my daughter. In my courtyard he must build a garden with three fountains. The first must send forth gold, the second diamonds, and the third gemstones. This must be completed by tomorrow morning."

Once again, the crab instructed the woman to strike the courtyard ground three times with the golden rod. Having followed the crab's directions, the next morning a splendid garden appeared. The king had no choice but to set a wedding date for the marriage of the crab and his daughter.

In preparation, the crab gave the fisherman the golden rod and sent him to the black mountain. The fisherman knocked on the rock with the golden rod and a little man appeared.

The fisherman repeated the crab's words. "My master, the king, has sent me to tell you to send him the gilded cushion, his royal robes that glow like the sunrise, and the golden wedding dress adorned with precious jewels of rainbow colors."

The fisherman returned with these priceless items. Dressed in his golden robes, the crab sat on the cushion as the fisherman carried him into the castle. The crab presented his bride the royal wedding dress. The ceremony was short and the celebration even shorter, as the red-faced king would not look anyone in the eye.

When the new couple were alone, the crab revealed his secret to his young wife. He explained that he was the son of a great king under an enchantment that made him a crab by day but by night he could shape-shift into a man or an eagle at will. Then, he shed his shell and spent the night with his new bride. But at dawn's light, he sadly crawled back into his golden shell. Time passed and the princess grew fond of her enchanted crab. Instead of despising him, the royal family noticed that she gave the crab her loving attention. They spied on the couple to discover their secret but could not find out the answer to this strange matter.

After a year, the princess gave birth to a healthy son. Her mother urged the king to ask his daughter about this strange relationship with a crab. Did she want a new husband? But the princess replied, "It is he that I married and I will only have him."

The king did not listen. He ordered a tournament in her honor, inviting all the princes in the world to participate. He told her that if she should see a knight who pleased her, the king would grant her leave to marry that prince.

Upon learning of the tournament, the crab gave his fair bride the golden rod and told her to summon the little man to give her the crab's golden armor, his steed, and a silver apple. Upon delivery of the requested items, the crab waited until evening, then, as the prince, he dressed for the tournament.

Before he left, he warned his wife. "When you see me, do not betray who I am. As you watch from the window with your sisters, I will throw you a silver apple but if they ask who I am, deny that you know me or evil will come to us."

She promised and they embraced. As the tournament came to a close, the princess and her sisters watched as a knight approached the window and tossed a silver apple to the princess. She caught it but said nothing to her sisters as to the identity of the knight, her crab husband. The king was perplexed that his daughter seemed indifferent to the handsome princes. So, he ordered a second tournament.

Again the crab cautioned the princess not to give away his identity when he threw her a golden apple. She assured him she would not.

But before the prince left for the tournament, he said, "Today, you will betray me."

The princess exclaimed, "No, a thousand times no!"

That evening, the crab prince rode by the window where the princess, her mother, and sisters stood. He flung the golden apple to his wife and then galloped away.

The princess said nothing and her mother screamed at her, "Does no one please you? Not even that one?" In her rage, she slapped the princess to the floor.

The princess forgot herself and cried out, "That was my husband, the crab."

Her mother was shocked and angry that her daughter had not told her about the crab. She stormed into her daughter's chamber and found the golden crab shell on the floor. In disgust, the queen burned the crab shell to ashes in the fireplace. The princess waited for her husband, but he did not return. In her despair, the princess grew ill, refusing to eat. To improve her spirits, the king sought storytellers, for he knew his daughter loved to hear stories.

An old man came to the castle to tell the princess his tale. His adventure began by a stream where he dipped his crust of dry bread to soften it. A hungry dog snatched it from him and ran off. Cursing the mongrel, the old man followed until they reached a door. The dog pushed through it and the man chased him down a staircase leading to a palace. As he walked into the great hall, he saw a table set for twelve people. Suddenly, he heard a commotion and quickly hid behind a cupboard. With beating wings, twelve wondrous eagles descended into the hall. Then they turned three times withershins (counterclockwise) and transformed into men. The old man trembled as he watched the men raise their goblets of wine in a toast. One spoke in honor of his father, another to his mother, and a third spoke of his beloved wife but cursed her cruel mother who destroyed his golden shell. After they had their meal, the men turned deosil (clockwise) and became eagles once again, leaving the palace as they came. The old man hurried out of the strange palace and returned home.

The princess jumped up, her cheeks on fire. "Can you take me there?"

"Of course, your Highness." He said.

In the palace, the old man and the princess hid behind the cupboard. He bade her to silence as they waited for the return of the eagles. Soon the eagles flew in and changed into young men. The princess gasped as she recognized her husband, but the old man shook his head. She saw them seated with the wine glasses in hand. When her husband rose to make his toast, the princess gave a cry. She ran out to him and threw her arms about him.

He recognized her and said, "Now you know I spoke the truth when I told you that you would betray me. But you have found me and if you will stay with me for three months, the enchantment will be broken."

"Oh, yes," she cried. "I will stay with you!"

She told the old man to return to the castle and tell her parents the plan. The message confused and angered the king and queen.

After three months passed, the prince became a man, both day and night. Hand in hand, they returned to his palace where they lived in peace and much happiness. (And they never ate crabs or fish again).

Notes

Crabs are crustaceans that have a pair of claws they use to catch their prey. They are omnivores eating plant matter as well as other animals. Instead of skin, crabs have a thick protective exoskeleton. As they increase in size, they must shed their exoskeleton (called molting) and grow a larger shell. If a crab loses a leg, it can regenerate or regrow that leg from the nub that is left. Some but not all crabs walk sideways.

In the sky there is a constellation of stars named Cancer, which is Latin for "crab." The Greek mythological story of Cancer concerns Hercules who was battling the multiheaded Hydra, a monstrous serpent with nine heads. Hercules crushed the large crab who bit him on the foot during the fight. The Goddess Hera, who did not like Hercules, rewarded the crab by placing it among the stars.

—KB

The Fisherman and His Wife

A folktale from Germany

Once there was a fisherman and his wife who made a meager living from the sea. The fisherman would go out in his little boat and, sometimes, if he was lucky, return home with a few fish. But most often he came back with only one or even none.

One day, the fisherman hooked a huge flounder. He truly could not believe his good fortune, but as he hauled his catch into the boat, the fish said, "Let me go, fisherman, and you will not be sorry, for I am an enchanted fish. If you let me go, you will catch another fish today, and in the future you may call on me for a favor."

The fisherman did not hesitate, but threw the flounder back into the sea. As soon as the fish was out of sight another took its place in the net. The fisherman decided to go home and tell his wife about the wonderful thing that had happened to him that day.

She was happy when she saw the big fish, that he brought home, but even more excited when he told her the story of the enchanted flounder.

"Did you ask the fish for a wish?"

"Well, no. I didn't think of that," he replied. "He sent me this beautiful fish."

"Fish? We live in this miserable hut and you're satisfied with a fish? Go back and ask him for a better house, a nice cottage."

The man went back to the sea and called out to the fish.

> Enchanted flounder in the sea,
>
> I have a wish, please come to me.
>
> My wife asks a favor of you,
>
> So, to your promise, please be true.

No sooner had the words left the fisherman's mouth than the flounder came to the shore and lifted its head out of the water. "What do you want with me?"

"My wife asks if we could live in a nice house instead of the run-down hut we have now."

"Go home," said the flounder, "and you will be pleased."

When the man got home, the hut was gone and a beautiful, new cottage was standing in its place, with a white picket fence and a small shed in the back. The curtains and all the furniture were new, even the pots and pans.

"Are you content?" asked the fisherman.

"Perhaps," replied his wife.

A few weeks later the fisherman's wife told him that the garden was too small, the kitchen too cramped, the parlor too crowded, and the bed too narrow. "We need a manor house like the one a great merchant would own."

"I'm happy with our new cottage. It's fine for me," said the fisherman.

"But not for me. Now go to the flounder and get us a manor house."

The fisherman went back to the sea and called out to the fish.

> Enchanted flounder in the sea,
>
> I have a wish, please come to me.
>
> My wife asks a favor of you,
>
> So, to your promise, please be true.

The flounder came to the surface and asked the fisherman what he wanted. The poor man told the fish of his new request.

"Go home. She has what she wants," said the fish.

When the man got home, servants met him at the door to his grand new house. The walls were hung with paintings and tapestries. The furniture was made of oak. Candelabras lit every room, and crystal glasses and plates of silver adorned the dining room.

His wife seemed very pleased. So the fisherman asked her, "Are you content at last?"

"Perhaps," replied his wife.

A few weeks later the greedy woman was looking out her window at the countryside around their manor house. "Husband," she said, "wouldn't it be nice if all the land as far as we could see was ours? Go tell the flounder that we want to be king and queen of all these lands."

"You must be crazy," said the fisherman. "I do not want to be king."

"Fine then, just tell the flounder that I want to be queen and live in a fine palace."

The fisherman slowly walked back to the sea and called out to the fish.

> Enchanted flounder in the sea,
>
> I have a wish, please come to me.
>
> My wife asks a favor of you,
>
> So, to your promise, please be true.

The flounder came to the surface and asked the fisherman what he wanted. The tired man told the fish of his wife's new request to be queen.

"Go home. She has what she wants," said the flounder.

When the fisherman returned home, he found a palace with guards at the gates and servants running here and there. There were fountains and gardens and everything was made of gold.

His wife seemed very pleased. So the fisherman bravely asked her, "Now are you content?"

"Perhaps," replied his wife.

A few weeks later his wife was watching the sunrise and she said, "Being the queen is not enough. I want to be ruler of the universe. I want every creature to bow before me. I want to make the sun rise and set and command the stars to shine. I want all life to come from me. Now go and tell the flounder that I want to rule the universe."

The fisherman went back to the sea. He stood by the shore, looking over the waves. Finally, he called out to the fish.

> Enchanted flounder in the sea,
>
> I have a wish, please come to me.

My wife asks a favor of you,

So, to your promise, please be true.

The flounder came to the surface and asked, "What does your wife want now?"

"She wants to rule the universe and all living things. She wants to control the sun and moon and stars."

"Go back to your wife. She has what she deserves."

When the fisherman got home, his wife was standing in front of their old hut. The old fisherman was pleased. As for his wife, if she was not, she was at least a bit wiser.

Notes

Flounders are native to the waters of Europe, where this story originates, and range from the White Sea in the north to the Mediterranean and Black Sea in the south. Unlike many other fish, flounders have very flat bodies designed to rest on the floor of a body of water. They are oval in shape and have both of their eyes located on the side of their body that faces upward. They are nocturnal and eat at or near the bottom of the seas and oceans where they live.

—DK

Emelya, the Fool

A folktale from Russia

Once there were three brothers. Now, the two older brothers were wise men, but Emelya, the youngest, was a fool. All he liked to do was sleep in the winter as he lay on the top shelf of the huge stove, and in the summer he stretched out in the shade of a big oak tree. Now, one day the two older brothers left home on a business trip and told their younger brother to obey their wives as if they were his mothers. They promised to bring Emelya a new shirt, caftan, and boots in his favorite color red if he obeyed them. He agreed to respect his sisters-in-law and do their bidding.

As soon as his brothers left, Emelya crawled back on top of the stove and fell asleep. One of his sisters-in-law saw him and said, "Emelya, what are you doing? Do you want the gifts your brothers promised you or not? Now go and fill the pails full of water."

Emelya went down to the river and started to fill the pails with water. Just as he was filling the last one, a pike jumped into the pail. "This is wonderful. I can cook this fish and have a good supper."

The pike spoke and said, "Don't be foolish. If you set me free, you will be happy."

"Why will I be happy?"

"Because everything you say will come true. For example say, 'By the pike's wish pails go home and take your usual place in the kitchen.'"

Emelya said the words and the pails all grew little wooden legs and ran home, through the door and into the kitchen. His sisters-in-law saw this and thought he wasn't quite as simple as everyone thought. Emelya came home and went straight to the top of the stove and fell asleep.

Now that the sisters knew that Emelya could command tasks to be done, they decided to take advantage of his magic. They told him that they needed more wood for the stove and for the woodpile. There would be no supper without wood for the stove. Emelya slowly rose and took two axes and sat in the sled. His sisters-in-law laughed and said, "You need to harness the horse you fool."

"By the pike's wish sled take me to the heart of the forest." And that's just what the sled did. Emelya and the sled started to move down the road without a horse. They gathered more and more speed until they came to the village and then they plowed through the crowd scattering women and children and men every which way throughout the village streets. People yelled and screamed and cursed but Emelya ignored them and continued down the road. Eventually the sled dove into the forest and came to a stop in the center of the woods. Emelya turned to the two axes and said, "By the pike's wish chop down a few trees and cut them into logs for the stove and pile them on the sled." The axes got to work and in no time the sled was filled with wood. As they approached the village, Emelya said, "By the pike's wish axes clear the way." The axes jumped up and flew through the air while people ran in terror as the sled barreled through the town.

When he got back home, the wood neatly jumped off the sled and stacked itself next to the backdoor. Emelya went back to sleep on top of the stove.

Now the people of the village sent word to the tsar that Emelya was a menace and that people were afraid of his reckless behavior. The tsar decided to send one of his men to Emelya and order him to come to the palace. When the tsar's man arrived, Emelya was still on top of the stove sleeping. When the messenger woke him and demanded that he come to see the tsar, Emelya said, "By the pike's wish I want the broom to sweep this man out of the house." And that's just what the broom did.

Now the townspeople went back to the tsar and told him that if he offered Emelya something in his favorite color red he would probably obey any order. The next messenger told Emelya that a fancy red coat was waiting for him if he visited the tsar. Emelya said, "By the pike's wish I want this stove to take me to the tsar's palace." And that's just what the stove did.

When Emelya arrived at the palace, he was immediately taken by the guards and brought before the tsar. As soon as the tsar's daughter set eyes on Emelya, she fell in love with him and he with her. The princess begged and pleaded for his life, and only to silence her, the tsar spared Emelya's life and had them married. But the tsar was still angry so he had them both put into a barrel and cast into the sea.

The barrel bobbed and floated in the sea for many hours until the princess said, "Can't you use your magic to get us ashore safely?"

"Of course," said Emelya, "why hadn't I thought of that? By the pike's wish barrel take us safely to shore." And that's what the barrel did.

The princess said, "We will need some shelter."

"Why hadn't I thought of that? By the pike's wish have a palace built right across from the tsar's palace and have us brought there." And that's what happened.

The tsar saw a palace where there had not been one a moment before and went to see who was living there. When he saw his daughter and Emelya, he was so happy that he forgave them both and they lived in happiness and prosperity for a very long time.

By the pike's wish it came to pass. And so it did.

Notes

The stoves in Russia are huge and often the elderly or children will sleep on the shelf on the top of the stove. They are used not only for baking and cooking but also for keeping the house warm. The pike is one of the oldest fish in the world and can be found in North America, Europe, and across Asia. They are a fresh water fish that lives in ponds, lakes, and rivers.

—DK

The Little Red Fish and the Clog of Gold

A folktale from Iraq

There once was a fisherman who lived neither here nor there. When his wife died, he was left with a young daughter to care for. The neighbor, a widow with her own daughter of about the same age as his, would often come over and help him. She would clean the house and fix enough meals to last him and his child for a couple of days. She would comb the girl's hair and say, "Am I not like a mother to you?"

But if ever the idea of marriage came up, the fisherman would always declare that he would never marry again. "I know that no stepparents would ever treat a child of another like they would their own."

As the girl grew a bit older, she noticed the loneliness in her father's eyes. He toiled to provide for them both and also keep the house clean. And though she was a help to him, she was still too young to do many of the chores. She would often say to him, "Why not marry the woman next door? She treats me as if I were her own daughter."

They say that water will wear away a stone if it flows over it long enough, and so, one day the fisherman and the neighbor were married. But they had not been married long before the new stepmother noticed how the fisherman favored his own child over hers. She noticed how much he loved and pampered his daughter. She also saw that her new stepdaughter was very pretty and quick with a needle and thread, while her own daughter was dull and plain and had few skills at all.

After a few weeks the new wife began to treat her stepdaughter very differently. She would not let her wash her face, hands, or feet and only fed her the sparse leftovers from the meals she prepared for the rest of the family.

While the neglected child did all the work, her stepmother's daughter did nothing all day. She sat idly by and watched as her stepsister toiled around her. The fisherman's daughter did not say anything to her father. She thought to herself, "I picked up the scorpion with my own hand so I'll save myself with my own mind."

One of the many chores that the young girl did daily was to go down to the river and bring home the fish her father had caught that day. As she walked up the bank of the river with a basket of fish, she heard the small voice come from a little red fish that lay under three large catfish.

"Child with such patience to endure
I beg you now my life secure
Throw me back into the water
And you will always be my daughter."

At first the child was afraid of the voice but she ran down to the water's edge and threw the red fish back into the river. She called after the fish, "Do a good deed, for even if it's like throwing money into the sea, in God's sight it is not lost." The fish called back to her,

"No kindness is ever in vain
For a new mother you have gained
Come to me when you are sad
And I shall be here to make you glad."

The young girl went home and gave her stepmother the three catfish. When her father returned, he asked his wife if she had cooked the four fish he had sent home. The stepmother was furious when she heard this, but the father gently asked his daughter about the fourth fish.

"I must have dropped it back into the river. It was only a small red fish."

The father dismissed it but the stepmother scolded her and sent her back to the river to look for the lost fish. She told the girl that she would curse her if she did not bring it back. So the girl walked back to the bank of the river and called out,

"Red fish my mother and nurse
Come quick to me and ward off a curse."

The fish came close to the child and comforted her in a soothing voice. "Reach inside my mouth," she said, "and take this piece of gold to your stepmother. Tell her you found it near the place where you lost the fish." So the girl did as the red fish told her and nothing was said about the missing fish again. Whenever the girl needed someone to talk to the red fish was there, always listening, always saying the right words to console the child.

The years passed and the two stepsisters grew into young women. Nothing had changed. The stepmother's daughter still did nothing around the house, while the fisherman's daughter did all the work and received nothing but scorn for her labors.

One day it was announced that the only daughter of the master of the Merchants' Guild was to be wed. All the women in the town would gather for the day of the bride's henna, a time when the bride's hands, feet, and arms were decorated with fine, red designs for the wedding ceremony. Every mother with unwed daughters brought them to the party to be seen by the mothers of unwed sons. Marriages were often arranged on such a day.

The fisherman's wife scrubbed her daughter and dressed her in the finest clothes and hurried off to the merchant's house for the celebration. She told the fisherman's daughter to stay behind and fetch water and sweep the floors.

As soon as the mother and daughter were gone, the girl ran down to the river and poured out her heart to the red fish. "You shall go to the bride's henna," said the red fish, "and you will be seated at a place of honor." She dove down into the water and came up with a small bundle. "Here is everything you'll need for the party. Just make sure you leave the celebration before your stepmother rises to go home."

Inside the bundle the young woman found a pearl comb for her hair and golden clogs, open-back slippers for her feet. There was a gown of the finest silk, the color of clover, stitched with threads of gold and decorated with diamond sequins. She washed herself and, dressed as a fine wealthy young noble woman, made her way to the bride's henna.

When the fisherman's daughter arrived, all the women of the town were there seated according to their standing in the community. At the sight of the beautiful new guest all conversation stopped. Everyone thought she must be the governor's daughter or perhaps even a member of the royal family. She was led to a cushion in the middle of the gathering, the place of honor, and treated to the finest foods. Her stepmother and stepsister were seated in the back of the room with the wives of peddlers. She saw the resemblance to her own stepdaughter but dismissed it. "They say that everyone has at least one double and so it must be."

Before the gathering was ended the fisherman's daughter rose and thanked the hostess saying, "May you and yours be blessed with Allah's bounty." As the light began to fade, she hurried to cross the stream that flowed into the king's garden. But she stumbled on the dark bridge and lost one of her golden clogs in the water below. Taking off her other clog, she ran home as quickly as she could. She took off her fine dress, pulled the pearl comb from her hair, and hid it with her golden clog under a woodpile. Then she rubbed dirt into her face and hands and began to sweep the floors, just as her stepmother entered the room.

Now the lost golden clog swirled away down the stream until it came to a quiet pool, not far from the palace. The next day, when the prince brought his horse to the pool, it shied away from the water and would not drink. So he bent over and reached into the water to find out what might have frightened his horse. When his hand touched the clog, half buried in the mud, he pulled it from the bottom of the pool. As he rode back to the stables, he turned the golden clog over and over in his hands, wondering who might have lost it. Was she a person of royal blood or a great man's daughter? Who else might wear such a fine, golden clog? He had to know.

His mother the queen noticed him in the garden looking at the slipper. "My son," she asked, "is there something that weighs on your mind?"

"I found this golden clog in the watering pool. I am captivated by the idea of who might own it. I've never met a girl who could make me happy in marriage. Perhaps the owner of this slipper is the one. Please mother, can you help me find her?"

The queen knew her son well and promised that she would use all her wiles to find the owner of the golden clog. The very next day she began her search, going from house to house and having every unwed young lady try on the clog. Every evening the prince asked if she had found the owner of the golden clog and every evening she would say, "No, not yet my son, but soon."

After weeks and weeks of searching, it was rumored that the queen would visit the homes of the fisher folk. The stepmother bathed her daughter and washed her hair with henna. Then she perfumed her and dressed her in a fine dress. But still she could not compare in any way with the fisherman's daughter. Even though she was dirty and thin, through the grace of Allah and the kindness of the red fish, she glowed with goodness and beauty. The stepmother dragged her out into the yard and pushed her into the bake house. Then she rolled a large stone in front of the opening. "You'll stay here and not make a sound if you know what is good for you."

Now the rooster that lived next door saw what was happening and flew to the river. He told the red fish what the stepmother had done. The red fish carefully explained exactly what the rooster was to do. The rooster flew back and perched on the fence between the two houses and waited.

The queen arrived at the house and called for the young women who lived there to come out and present themselves. The fisherman's wife brought her own daughter out and they bowed to the queen. The golden clog was placed next to her foot and it was obvious that it was not hers. Just then the rooster started to crow.

"Let the king's wife know
That the nasty one is the one they show
The sweetest beauty lies down below."

The stepmother tried to shoo the bird away but the queen had heard the words and had her servants search for the other daughter. When they found the bake house and rolled the stone away, the fisherman's daughter seemed to shine like diamonds in moonlight. And the clog was a perfect fit.

"From this day on," said the queen, "this girl is betrothed to my son the prince. The marriage procession shall arrive on Friday to bring her to the palace. Have her ready." The queen handed the stepmother a purse of gold and left.

The stepmother was furious that her plans had all gone wrong. To think that the fisherman's daughter would marry the prince while her own child was left at home was too much for her to bear. She took the gold and went to the herbalist in the market, where she paid him to prepare a poison so strong that it would destroy the body from the inside out. Then she asked for an ointment that would smell like a rotting corpse. Last, she had him mix up arsenic and lime to treat the girl's hair so it would all fall out. She would make sure the prince would send her stepdaughter home right away.

On Friday, the cruel woman washed the girl's hair with henna mixed with arsenic and lime. She spread the ointment over her body and had her drink the potion. The wedding procession came, and she was taken away to the palace.

When she was presented to the prince, the fisherman's daughter didn't smell like a rotting corpse but instead the fragrance of roses filled the room. Her hair, instead of falling out, felt like golden silk. Instead of her body rotting from the inside out, golden coins fell from her fingertips and spread out across the room, covering the carpets.

The stepmother waited outside the palace gates to watch the queen and her son throw the fisherman's daughter out in disgrace. But instead, news came that the couple were deep in love and happy at finding each other.

Word spread of the rose fragrance and the coins that fell from her fingertips. The master of the Merchants' Guild had a second son who wanted to marry the sister of the new princess. The stepmother gave her the same potion, washed her hair in arsenic and lime, and covered her with the foul smelling ointment. But instead of the smell of roses the odor of rotting flesh filled the wedding hall and her hair fell out in clumps while her body began to rot from the inside out, filling the hall with obnoxious smells. She was sent home in disgrace.

The prince and the fisherman's daughter lived in peace and harmony for all their days, blessed with many children and a love that never died. The red fish came to live in the pool on the palace grounds and counseled their children as it once had counseled the princess.

Notes

This folktale from Iraq belongs to the Cinderella family of stories. Henna, also called the henna tree or the Egyptian privet is a flowering plant. The leaves of henna are used to make the dye, also called henna, that is used to create temporary artistic tattoos. Henna has been used for 6,000 years as a cosmetic dye. The temporary tattoos are an important addition to a woman's appearance on special days.

—DK

The Grateful Alligators

A folktale from the USA

The Mississippi River is one of the great waterways in America. Before the era of the long barges that are seen on the river today, there were great riverboats, majestic palaces on water, that carried passengers and cargo. One day, a riverboat passenger, a man who had never traveled on the river before, was granted permission to visit the wheelhouse and observe the boat's progress. Now, the captain might command the boat, but the pilot steered the boat and was king of the wheelhouse. The pilot knew every inch of the river, where the waters were safe to maneuver and where the boat might run aground. This particular pilot was not only a seasoned veteran of the Mississippi, but also a man well-known for his honesty.

After a long period of silence, the passenger asked, "Are there many alligators on the river?"

"Not as many as there were before men started hunting them for their hides and meat," replied the pilot.

"So, there used to be a lot of them, back then?"

"Mister, I am known as an honest man, and I cannot tell a lie, but I once counted over a thousand gators for every mile from Vicksburg to New Orleans. Once, I even saw over three thousand gators on one big sandbar."

"Really, that many? It must have been hard to maneuver the boats down the river."

"Sir, we used to hurt so many of those poor creatures with our big paddle wheels that it would make a grown man cry to hear the pitiful beasts moaning in pain."

"That is remarkable. I don't doubt that it must have been hard."

"I used to work on a boat called *The Nancy Jane,* and her master was Captain Tom. That man was one of the kindest, gentlest men that ever worked this river. He used to carry a thousand bottles of salve and ointments for those poor beasts, and every time we hit a gator he would pour some medicine into the river water to ease their pain and help them heal. The gators knew of Captain Tom's kindness and they would rub up against *The Nancy Jane* and try to smile with those big toothy mouths. Tom would reach down and they would roll over just so he could rub their bellies. Those gators loved the old man."

"They did?" replied the passenger.

"Oh, yes sir, they did. One time we were going down the river and got stuck on a sandbar. We could not get that big boat to move one inch. When the alligators realized it was *The Nancy Jane,* hundreds of them came up on the sandbar and began to heave and shove. Finally the gators freed that boat and we steamed on down the river. I know it's hard to believe, but that is a fact."

"And I believe you," said the passenger.

"Well, thank you sir. I have never told a lie in my whole life. Yes, my mama raised me to be a truthful man, so I'll tell you about another time on *The Nancy Jane.* We were in a race with another riverboat, when our engines stopped working and there we were, dead in the water. Suddenly, hundreds of gators came along side. Captain Tom threw a towline overboard and those marvelous creatures grabbed that line in their mouths and towed us all the way up river to Vicksburg. You know, by golly, we won that race."

"Man, I wish I could have been there."

"Well, sir, I must say that it was a sad day when Captain Tom died for he was loved by man and beast alike. In fact, every gator on the Mississippi covered his left ear with black mud as a sign of mourning. They even followed *The Nancy Jane* down the river to New Orleans for his funeral, bellowing all the way."

The passenger felt a tear come to his eye as he heard about Captain Tom's death. He thanked the pilot and went down to the deck below.

The pilot turned back to his wheel, with a shake of his head and a smile on his face.

———————————

Notes

The word alligator probably comes from the Spanish "el lagarto," which means "the lizard," and was used by early Spanish explorers and settlers. Alligators are found in Louisiana and Florida as well as other coastal southern states. They usually live from thirty-five to fifty years, range in size from eight to fifteen feet long, and weigh as much as a thousand pounds. A group of alligators is called a congregation.

Riverboats were large ships propelled by steam-driven paddle wheels. They dominated the trade on the Mississippi for decades.

—DK

Section 4

Creatures Working Together

The Youth Who Made Friends
with the Beasts and the Birds

A myth from Peru

Back, far back, in the misty mountains of Peru, there lived a poor boy named Huathlacuri. While he did not even own so much as a cooking pot, he was rich in the ways of the natural world. He learned much wisdom from his father, Paricaca, who lived alone inside a giant eggshell on top of the mountain. Some believed that Paricaca was a shaman or wise man; some even thought he was a god.

Paricaca taught his son the ways of the birds and beasts and "to always be kind to the animals." Huathlacuri roamed unafraid among the cougars, foxes, snakes, buzzards, as well as the deer, tapirs, and armadillos because he spoke to them as friends. One day, a scarlet macaw told Huathlacuri of an unusual home of a rich man with a roof made of brightly colored feathers. Huathlacuri wanted to see this strange, wondrous house so he set out to find it. Along the way, he overheard two foxes gossiping about the illness that plagued this rich man. This only added to Huathlacuri's curiosity about the rich man and his extraordinary home.

Though he was dusty from his travel and his clothes worn and ragged, Huathlacuri, nonetheless, marched up to the feather-roofed house and knocked. A pretty girl, the rich man's youngest daughter, opened the door and Huathlacuri's heart skipped a beat. Taking a deep breath, he asked after her father. Though many a doctor tried to cure her father, the young woman told him, none had succeeded. Indeed, it seemed the rich man's health only grew worse.

"I can cure your father and in exchange," Huathlacuri said, his eyes shining with love, "I would like very much to have you as my wife, if you will have me."

The daughter looked at the scruffy young man. He had a gentleness about him that gave her pause.

"I will take you to my father and then we shall see," she said.

Huathlacuri made the same offer to the rich man for his daughter. The sick man was desperate—he was willing to try anything and make any promise.

Huathlacuri said, "Your wife is under a wicked spell by a sorcerer who takes the form of a serpent. She feeds the snake your maize and gives it your gold. There is a two-headed toad living under the grinding stone who serves the snake as its master. I will kill them both and you will recover from this evil."

Under the grinding stone, they found a two-headed toad and the snake sunning nearby. The toad and reptile were destroyed, freeing the rich man and his wife from the evil spell.

Wedding plans for Huathlacuri and the rich man's lovely daughter were underway when the girl's brother-in-law objected. He was embarrassed to have such a poor, shabby man be part of the family, so he proposed a series of contests between Huathlacuri and himself. The loser of the contests would be disgraced and have to leave the family. The rich man agreed to hold the contest as long as Huathlacuri consented. Huathlacuri saw that the brother-in-law would not give him peace and agreed to the contest. The first challenge was a dancing and drinking contest.

Huathlacuri sought help from his friends, the foxes. The fox gave him a magic flute of five pipes and the vixen provided him a gourd filled with *chichi*, a corn water drink. In gratitude, Huathlacuri gave food to the foxes.

With the magical pipes and gourd, Huathlacuri could outdance and outdrink the haughty brother-in-law. Unwilling to give up, the brother-in-law proposed yet another contest. Knowing that Huathlacuri was poor, he wanted to see which of them could come to the feast dressed in the finest attire. Paricaca came to his son's aid and gave him the beautiful skin of a golden cougar to wear. The tawny fur glowed like the rising sun, impressing everyone. Huathlacuri won that contest too.

But the stubborn brother-in-law would not accept defeat. The next contest was to see who could build the best house in the shortest time. The brother-in-law ordered all his servants to help build the house and with many hands, the house quickly rose up. Soon, it only needed a roof.

Working alone, Huathlacuri had barely started his foundation. Once again, Huathlacuri sought help from his animal friends. Overnight the wildcats, tapirs, monkeys, birds, and other beasts worked steadily to build his house. Then the cougars spotted the brother-in-law's llamas saddled with straw ready to complete the roof and they ran toward the llamas with thunderous roaring. Frightened, the timid llamas ran this way and that, scattering the straw to the four winds. Once again, Huathlacuri was victorious.

It was time for the wedding, still the brother-in-law interfered. Paricaca told Huathlacuri to end this conflict between them. When the brother-in-law proposed a running contest, Huathlacuri growled at him. The frightened brother-in-law turned away to run and as he did, Huathlacuri touched him, transforming him into a deer that quickly disappeared into the woods.

Huathlacuri and his wife lived happily in their new home. His father's words, "always be kind to the animals," proved to be wise words indeed.

Notes

Huathlacuri is a healer or curandero *in the shamanistic tradition. His kindness and respect for the natural world give him the magical ability to communicate with animals. Shamans have animal helpers. They use mind-altering herbal drinks and ritual to effect cures or magically change something. The shaman's knowledge is passed down to relatives just as Paricaca gave Huathlacuri advice and help. In the story, Huathlacuri dances (perhaps ritualistically), drinks a magical liquid given to him by his fox helpers, and transforms his brother-in-law into a deer. These are in keeping with the powers and behavior of a shaman or witch doctor in South America.*

Paricaca lives on the top of the mountain in an eggshell. In the Andean cosmology, the universe is seen as an egg. The egg also represents the soul. Paricaca could be seen as representing the divine as well as a healer.

—KB

The King's Youngest Son

A folktale from the Republic of Georgia

In olden days, when many kings reigned throughout the world, there lived one king, who after a long illness became blind. He sent his three sons to find a doctor who could cure him. Many a doctor tried, but no one knew what to do. Finally, one day, a physician examined the blind monarch and said that the blood of a certain scarlet-colored fish sprinkled over his eyes might cure him.

Word went out to all the fishermen that whoever caught such a fish would be handsomely rewarded. Weeks passed and finally an old fisherman caught a glistening ruby-colored fish and brought it to the palace. The king was sleeping so his servant took the bucket with the beautiful fish and left it in the hall outside the king's bedchamber.

After his morning lessons, golden-eyed Tholiorko, the king's youngest son, went to check on his father. In the bucket, he spied the magic fish. He knew the scarlet fish was meant for the king but Tholiorko was kind-hearted and felt it would be wicked to kill such a magnificent fish. So he took the bucket and returned the fish to the river.

The fish called out, "Someday I will repay your kindness. Call me if you ever need help," and with a splash of its shimmering red tail, the fish disappeared into the deep churning waters.

The youngest son's deed was reported and the king was outraged.

"Tholiorko, you have betrayed me! I banish you forever from this kingdom. You are no longer my son and I never want to hear you again."

With tears in his eyes, Tholiorko ran into the great forest. As he moved deeper into the woods, he saw a panicked deer racing toward him, pursued by baying hounds. The youth took pity and called to the deer.

"Come, I will help you," Tholiorko shouted.

The exhausted deer bowed her head and Tholiorko threw his arms around the animal's neck. As the hunters drew up, Tholiorko exclaimed, "This deer belongs to the king. I have trained and tamed it. Do not chase the animals in this forest again!"

The huntsmen noticed the youth's fine clothes and believed him. After they rode away, Tholiorko released the deer.

The deer said, "Someday I will repay your kindness. Call me if you ever need help."

On and on, Tholiorko walked. Suddenly, he came upon an eagle caught in a fishing net in the branches of a tree. Gently cutting away the ropes from the struggling creature, he freed the mighty bird.

"Someday I will repay your kindness," it said. "Call me if you ever need help." The eagle soared into the sky and was gone.

Tholiorko crossed a stream and came upon a small red fox with its leg caught in a snare. At once he released the fox from the cruel trap.

The fox said, "Someday I will repay your kindness. Take this long red hair and roll it between your hands if you ever need help."

The fox plucked a long hair from his tail and gave it to the boy. Tholiorko carefully put the hair in his pocket and thanked the fox. With a graceful leap, the fox disappeared into the woods.

Eventually, Tholiorko found himself outside the forest standing before a crystal glass castle, shining brilliantly in the summer sun. As he walked into the courtyard, his eyes grew wide. The ground was littered with dead young men. A servant told Tholiorko that the beautiful princess decreed she would only marry a man whom she could not find, that is, a man who could hide himself from her. The dead men on the courtyard were failed suitors cast from the top of the castle to their death.

The princess sat on her throne as Tholiorko approached. He was charmed by her appearance and asked to be given a chance to gain her hand in marriage.

She consented but warned him, "If you fail to hide yourself in a place I cannot discover, then you must give up your life."

"I will agree, if you promise to give me four opportunities to hide," replied Tholiorko.

The princess looked at the handsome young man and cocked her head to the side. She found the request unusual and felt challenged by the game.

"I will grant your request," she said with a smile dancing in her eyes.

Tholiorko returned to the river and called out to the magic scarlet fish. At once, the shimmering ruby fish appeared and agreed to help. The fish grew enormous and then swallowed Tholiorko. It swam to the deepest part of the sea to hide. The next morning the princess took out her enchanted mirror and gazed at it. Through the mirror she looked into the forests, mountains, and plains. She did not find Tholiorko. Then she looked into the sky and the wind but she did not see him. Next she looked into the lakes, rivers, and the seas. There, she finally found Tholiorko in the belly of a red fish and she sat back satisfied.

The next day, Tholiorko came to claim the princess as his bride, but she told him that she had found him at the bottom of the sea in the belly of a scarlet fish. After the princess dismissed him, her lips curled in a smile. She was impressed with Tholiorko's unique hiding place.

Tholiorko hurried to the forest and called out for the deer. Rustling through the bushes, the fleet deer appeared. Happy to help, she bent down for Tholiorko to climb on her back. She ran like the wind for a long while until they came to the seventh mountain. In a small cave, Tholiorko slept while the deer covered the opening with her body.

The following morning, the princess took out her magical mirror and looked deeply into it. She searched the waters, the sky, and finally the earth. Her tired eyes strained to find the young man. At last, in a cave on the seventh mountain, she discovered him hidden by a tawny deer.

Tholiorko was certain he had hidden himself well, but back at the castle, the princess revealed his hiding place.

"You have two more chances," she said. "Now go."

Determined to win, the youth called out to the eagle in a large field. Suddenly, the bird swooped down and grabbed Tholiorko in his talons. They soared into the blue until they reached the clouds. The king of the birds hid Tholiorko in a thick white cloud and shielded him with his wings.

Once again, the princess looked for Tholiorko. Hours passed as she poured across the land, the oceans, and the horizon. At last she looked toward the sun and saw the cumulus cloud covering Tholiorko and the great eagle shielding him. She rubbed her red eyes and smiled for she found the young man to be quite special.

As she described Tholiorko's hiding place, he frowned. He had only one more chance! In the forest, the desperate Tholiorko rubbed the red fox hair between his hands. Instantly, the little fox appeared ready to help. The fox called more foxes and they set to digging out a tunnel beneath the room of the princess.

When it was completed, the fox said, "You must stay underneath her room until she gives up and breaks the mirror. Then, push out the floorboards into her chamber and reveal yourself."

The next day, the princess took out her mirror and searched the four directions. Hours passed and her eyes grew tired and strained as she searched but could not find the young man. Again and again she reviewed the earth, the sky, and the seas but failed to see him. She did not eat, nor rest. Into the night, she sought him.

At last, she stood up and cried out, "I cannot find him anywhere! He has won."

In her irritation, she threw the mirror across the room where it broke into shards that vanished like smoke.

Tholiorko pushed his way through the floor. "At last you are mine," he said, "and I am yours."

Offering him her hand, the princess smiled. They celebrated with a marriage feast that lasted a week. By day and by night, the happy pair lived long in peace and happiness.

> *Leave a good deed on a stone by the way, Thou'lt find it again after many a day.*

—Mingrelian proverb

Notes

The Republic of Georgia is a small country sandwiched between Russia and Turkey and borders the Black Sea to the west. The Caucasian Mountains stand to the north, while the Armenian Mountains bound to the south. The Republic of Georgia is slightly smaller than the state of South Carolina and has a population of about 4.6 million. This Mingrelian story comes from the Samegrelo region of the Republic of Georgia. At one time, the Mingrelians believed in wood spirits and other pagan deities. Tholiorko's shamanistic ability to understand the animals reflects the story's pagan roots.

—KB

The Helpful Animals

A Burmese (Myanmar) folktale

Many years ago, in a time when memory was young, there lived a widow and her only son, Po. Now that he had grown to be a young man, the time had come for him to take his father's place and look after his inheritance.

"Po, you must go out and learn the ways of the world," his mother said. "On your journey, may you acquire wisdom."

With a sack of silver coins and two servants to accompany him, Po eagerly began his adventure. He would show his mother that he was sensible and could manage his money well.

Along the path, they came across a man who had a sickly dog with its tail between its legs. The man scolded the half-starved dog and yanked on its leash causing the dog to whimper. Po remembered his Buddhist teachings and felt compassion toward the miserable dog.

"How much for your dog?" Po asked.

The man looked Po up and down and said, "One hundred coins for my dog."

Without a word, Po paid the greedy man the silver coins. Then he sent his servant and the mutt home with instructions for his mother to feed and care for the dog. Po's mother was very surprised at Po's request and the amount of money he paid for the ailing creature, but she did as he requested. With time, the dog recovered his health and fiercely guarded the gate, barking whenever strangers approached.

The next day, Po saw a man carrying a scrawny, wretched cat. Immediately he sought to help the poor creature.

"Will you take one hundred pieces of silver for your cat?" asked Po.

The man smiled at Po. He was no fool and happily sold the worthless cat for the huge sum of money offered. Po sent his second servant home with the cat for his mother to nurse back to health. Confused, the widow shrugged but gave the cat a warm bed and a bowl of milk. Soon the cat was chasing mice and Po's mother was glad to have the cat.

Walking in the woods one day, Po heard a whimper of pain. He found a mongoose with his foot caught in a trap. Gently, Po released the injured paw and wrapped the creature in his coat to carry him home. His mother bandaged the foot and fed the sleek mongoose a rice gruel with raw eggs. With time and care, his paw healed nicely. Po's mother saw that the wild animal needed to return to the woods. She opened the gate and he ran like a monsoon wind into the forest.

The wily creature came to a clear fresh water pond. This was a special little lake where the genie's daughter liked to swim. The mongoose paused to drink. He thought about the kindness of Po and his mother and wanted to repay them. As he looked into the clear water, his keen eyes spotted a glowing golden ring with a pink pearl toward the edge of the pond. The mongoose knew of the ring's genie power. Grasping the magic ring in his mouth, he ran back to Po's house.

"This is my thanks to you," he said in his squeaky voice. "Here is a genie's ring. Turn it once around your finger. Wish for whatever your heart desires and it will be yours. Never, ever take the ring off or bad luck will come to you!"

Po thanked the mongoose for the precious gift and the mongoose sprinted back to the woods. Turning the ring, Po wished for a palace fit for a king and a pagoda with seven golden eaves in honor of Buddha. In the blink of an eye, there stood the palace and pagoda. Inside the palace were servants, fine clothes for Po and his mother, and a chest of gold, silver, and jewels.

The king of the land got word of this wondrous palace and pagoda. He was looking for a proper husband for his daughter and went to visit the master of the palace. Impressed not only with Po's fortune, the king was also taken with his gentle, kind ways. The lovely princess readily agreed to marry Po, who felt himself a lucky man to marry such a charming and beautiful woman.

They lived happily in the golden palace and their love grew with each new day. One afternoon, a monk dressed in saffron robes came and asked to spend the night. The princess was happy for a learned monk's company but the man was really a thief in disguise. He recognized the magic ring on Po's finger and asked the princess about it.

"I see your husband wears a beautiful pearl ring fit for royalty. Does he let you wear it too?" the false monk asked.

The princess looked puzzled at him. "It is his ring, not mine."

"But if he loved you, he would give you the ring to wear. For the pink pearl is like a lotus flower and a lovely lady like you deserves beautiful things." the monk said slyly. "Maybe he loves the ring more than you?"

"Oh no, that is not so, and I will prove it to you before you leave," she declared.

The princess went to Po and asked him if she might wear the ring tomorrow when he would be away on business.

"It will remind me of you, my love," she said.

Po smiled, he could not refuse his pretty wife, but made her promise not to take it off her finger or show it to anyone. He did not tell her of the ring's magical powers.

The next morning the princess held out her hand triumphantly for the monk to see the pearl ring on her finger.

"Ah, it is exquisite, but what is this on it?" the false monk said. "Please give me the ring that I may examine it closer."

The unsuspecting princess gave him the ring. The thief put the ring on him finger and turned himself into a black bird. The princess watched in horror as the crow flew to an island across the sea and out of reach of their small boats.

Tearfully, the princess told Po his ring was stolen by the false monk. The cat heard the bad news and decided to try to return the ring to his kind friend. The cat knew of the genie's favorite pond and ran into the woods until she found it. As luck would have it, the genie's daughter was bathing and her pink pearl necklace sat on top of her clothing by the edge of the water. The cat quickly snatched the lustrous necklace and hid it under broad green leaves for he knew the daughter could not return to her magical home without the special pink pearls.

The cat called out, "I will tell you where your necklace is hidden if you will part the sea waters to the island where the thief lives."

The agreement was made and a dry path was made to the island. The cat raced to the island and found the thief asleep. Gently, the cat removed the ring and then fled back to Po.

"Here is your ring," said the cat. "It is my way of thanking you for saving me from starvation."

Po stroked the cat. "I thank you, cat," he said and ordered a bowl of milk for the faithful creature.

Time passed and happiness returned to the palace. Po never removed his ring, but word spread among thieves of the magic ring. One night, a band of robbers came to the palace gate. The dog, barking a warning, lunged at the largest thief, biting him viciously. The other robbers were frightened of the fearsome dog and ran away with the huge man. The dog had saved Po and his family.

Po wished to show his gratitude to the animals so he gathered the dog, cat, and mongoose. He said, "Mongoose brought me good fortune with this ring and cat brought the stolen ring back to me. Dog bravely protected me and my family from a band of robbers. I am most thankful to my animal friends. You will always have food and shelter here, for you are my family too."

With his sharp teeth and keen eyes, the mongoose kept the snakes out of the palace garden. The cat hunted the rats and mice, while the dog guarded the palace gate. Together, they all lived in peace and much happiness.

Have compassion for all beings, rich and poor alike; each has their suffering. Some suffer too much, others too little.

—Buddha

Notes

Myanmar (formerly known as Burma) is located in southeastern Asia with its southwest border on the Andaman Sea. In size, it is slightly smaller than the state of Texas. It borders China, India, Laos, Thailand, and Bangladesh and has a population of over 55 million.

Most of the people of Myanmar are Buddhists. This religion has been a part of their history for close to 2,000 years. Refraining from killing or harming other living beings is a fundamental principle in Buddhism. Thus, Po's compassion toward the animals he rescued was a reflection of his religious upbringing. Buddhist monks are revered in Burmese culture, so Po's wife understandably trusted the false monk.

—KB

The Three Girls and the Johnnycakes

An Appalachian folktale

O nce, on the far side of yesterday, there lived a poor woman with her three grown daughters. One day the eldest daughter spoke up.

"Mammy, it's time for me to go out into the wide world and make my own living. Could you fix me some food to take along?"

Her mother fried up two johnnycakes made of cornmeal and then said to her eldest daughter,

"Would you druther have the big johnnycake with my curse or the little one with my blessing?"

Well now, the eldest thought she would be walking a long way, so curse or no, she said,

"I'll just take me that big one."

She wrapped her johnnycake up in her new Sunday shawl and began her walk through the woods. By and by, she grew hungry and tired. As she sat eating on a moss-covered log, birds and other animals gathered around her looking hungry and pitiful. But she waved them away saying,

"Go git your own food! There's only enough for me." She finished the big johnnycake, licking her fingers to get all the crumbs.

Soon she came to a house where she asked for work. The woman of the house hired her to watch over the body of a dead man that was stretched out on the kitchen table.

"That there is my dead brother," said the woman. "He's bewitched. I've been up with him day and night, so tonight I've gotta get some sleep.

If you can sit with him all night and stay awake, I'll pay you a peck* of gold, a peck of silver, and a bottle of ointment so powerful it can even cure the dead.

The girl thought it shouldn't be so hard to do and agreed. While it was still daylight, she tried to sleep. Her bed was soft, covered with a warm quilt, but all she did was toss and turn. She never slept a wink. That night, when it grew dark, the eldest daughter went into the kitchen to sit by the dead man. The woman had gone to bed to sleep. It was not long before the eldest daughter's eyelids grew heavy and she dozed off. When the dead man's sister woke up and found the girl sleeping, she whacked her on the head and killed her. The sister dragged the girl's body outside and tossed it into the holler.†

Time passed and the eldest daughter never returned home. So, the second daughter asked her mammy for a johnnycake. Just like the eldest, she chose the bigger cake with the curse, and she met with the same end as her dead elder sister.

Now the youngest of the three girls, Mary, decided to go look for her older sisters and asked her mother for a johnnycake.

"Well, Mary," her mother asked, "do you want my blessing and the pinch of a cake or the bigger cake and my curse?"

"Why, I'll just take your blessing, Mammy, with this here little johnny-cake," Mary replied.

"Alright," her mother said. "May you find both your fortune and your two sisters. Be safe and mind your manners."

Mary kissed her mammy goodbye and started her journey with her johnny-cake wrapped in an old threadbare shawl. In the forest, she stopped to eat. When the hungry birds and other animals gathered around her, Mary scattered the crumbs for them on the ground and they all had enough to eat. Later that afternoon, Mary and her forest friends came to the dead man's house. Mary knocked and asked for a job. The dead man's sister offered her gold, silver, and a bottle of powerful ointment if Mary would watch the bewitched brother through the night.

So Mary napped on a soft bed, curled up in a warm quilt until night came. Then she lit a candle and sat down by the dead man to sew. As her eyes grew heavy, the night birds perched on the windowsill and sang to keep her awake. Then, at about midnight, the dead man sat up.

Mary quickly stood up beside him and said, "You stay dead or I'm gonna beat you with this switch."

The bewitched man made a face like he ate something sour and then lay back down on the table. A little while later, he popped up again, so Mary whipped him with a hazel switch until he lay down. The third time the dead man sat up, he jumped right off the table and ran into the forest with Mary and her animal friends chasing after him. The wolf carried Mary on his back, while the rabbit and opossum kept tripping the dead man until he finally landed hard on the ground and stayed dead. With the help of the critters, Mary carried the man's body back to the house and collected her wages—a peck of gold, a peck of silver, and a bottle of ointment that could even cure the dead.

Then, the clever fox took Mary to the holler where her older sisters lay dead. Mary rubbed the powerful ointment on them and watched their ashen faces turn pink and healthy again. Back home, their mammy was overjoyed to see all three of her daughters. The gold and silver Mary had earned kept the family in comfort for a long while.

Notes

*A peck is about two dry gallons, in other words, a lot of money!

†"holler" means a hollow or small valley.

Johnnycakes or journey-cakes are a fried or baked flatbread usually made with ground corn, salt, and water. Early European settlers learned how to make this quick, filling bread from the Native Americans. Johnnycakes were a staple food at the time because cornmeal was cheap and the cakes were easy to prepare and cook.

Appalachia is a region in Eastern United States that follows along the Appalachian Mountains. In the early eighteenth century, the area was settled by Scotch-Irish immigrants as well as Germans. This story has its roots in a Scottish folktale but the animal helpers were introduced into the story by the Appalachian tellers.

—KB

The Queen Bee

A Germanic folktale

Once there was, twice there was, and once there was not a time when two princes, rough and reckless, sought adventure. Their wicked ways kept them from returning home so their youngest brother, Wilford, went in search of them. When he found his older brothers, they teased and mocked him. They thought themselves more clever and resourceful than their fool of a younger brother.

As the three traveled, the brothers came across a large, sandy anthill teaming with industrious tiny creatures. The oldest brother wanted to stomp on the ant's home, while the other brother planned to squash the fleeing ants under his boots.

But Wilford stopped them. "They have done nothing to you," he said. "Let them be. I won't let you destroy them."

Wilford stood between his brothers and the anthill, his hands fisted. The brothers laughed and threw a stone at Wilford and then continued their journey.

Later in the afternoon, a crystal lake shimmered in the sunlight as a family of ducks glided across it. Wilford's brothers wanted to hunt the ducks even though they had plenty of food. To the older princes, killing animals just for sport was fun.

"Let them be in peace!" Wilford exclaimed. "This is their home."

The afternoon was fading toward dusk and they needed to move on, so they left the ducks alone. Soon they came to a huge tree where bees were swarming. In the elbow of the trunk, they saw a hive dripping with honey.

The older brothers wanted to smoke out the bees so they could steal the honey.

"It is wrong to steal their food," Wilford said. "Leave them in peace. Besides, you cannot carry away the sticky, dripping honey."

Dusk was upon them, so the older princes decided to search for shelter. The three brothers came to a strange castle made of granite with stone horses in the stable, stone chickens in the coop, and stone cows in the barn, but not a breathing person to be found.

They wandered through the castle until they came to a door with three key-holed locks. Each peered through a keyhole and saw a gray dwarf wearing a red knitted cap. The oldest called to him, but he did not move. Knocking, the middle brother called to the little man, but he did not respond. When Wilford appealed to the dwarf, he quietly rose from his chair and unlocked the door.

Without a word, he led them into a dining room with a long table covered with savory foods and sweets. After they had eaten their fill, the little man silently escorted them each to a bed chamber.

The next morning the gray dwarf pointed to a stone tablet. The words carved on it described three tasks that had to be performed to break the spell cast on the granite castle. He pointed to the oldest brother and then to the first challenge on the tablet. To be successful, one had to complete the task of finding one thousand pearls hidden in a bed of thick, green moss before sunset. If the oldest brother failed, he would be transformed into a stone statue. The oldest brother searched all day but only found a few dozen pearls by dusk. As darkness fell, his skin turned ashen and then hardened into stone.

The following morning, Wilford's other brother set out to collect the pearls in the tangled moss. He found almost a hundred pearls by the time day melted into night. In the twilight, the color of his skin paled into a leaden gray and his limbs hardened like cement.

The next day it was Wilford's turn at the impossible task and by afternoon Wilford only had a couple of handfuls of the glossy pearls.

He sat on a rock and moaned with his head in his hands, "This is hopeless. What am I to do?"

A tiny voice replied, "You saved our home and now we will repay your kindness."

Wilford looked down and saw hundreds of ants in the moss carrying pearls to Wilford's bucket. Soon it was filled with a thousand shiny pearls.

Thanking the ants, Wilford turned to the next task, which was to fetch a key at the bottom of a deep lake. The key would open the tower bedroom of the three sleeping daughters of the king.

Standing beside the lake, Wilford sighed, "What am I to do?"

The duck family swam over to Wilford and offered to help. Diving repeatedly to the bottom, they searched until they finally found the missing key. Wilford thanked them and returned to the castle.

The next day Wilford learned the final challenge. Each of the king's three daughters was identical to the others with one exception. All had fallen into an enchanted slumber, but before this happened, one licked candy, another kissed sweet syrup, and the youngest tasted a spoonful of honey. Wilford's task was to choose the youngest who ate the honey. He groaned. How was he to know this simply by looking at their faces? Buzzing through the window came the queen bee.

"Your kindness saved us. I want to help you in return," she said.

The queen bee gently landed on the lips of each of the princesses. She found the honey on the lips of the youngest and finally Wilford was able to break the spell. The castle's inhabitants became flesh once again and celebrated.

The king rewarded Prince Wilford by giving him half his kingdom. The youngest princess became Wilford's wife and his brothers married her sisters. They lived happily and King Wilford ruled the land with kindness and wisdom.

Notes

Bees are one of the most important insects to mankind. They are essential in the pollination of crops ranging from almond trees to numerous fruits and vegetables that are worth $19 billion dollars to the U.S. economy. Bees have a complex social system and a sophisticated form of communication. Their waggle dance can tell other worker bees the direction, distance, and quality of food sources. The queen bee lives for about three years and lays up to fifteen hundred eggs a day during her lifetime.

The honeybee was brought over to the United States by the European immigrants. Today there is much concern over the drastic reduction of the bee population. Colony collapse disorder has many scientists, farmers, and politicians looking for ways to save the bees. Without their work as pollinators, agriculture will suffer and our food sources will be severely impacted.

—KB

The Two Stepsisters

A Norwegian folktale

Once upon a time, there were two stepsisters who were as different as night and day. The mother's daughter liked to loaf about and was rather thick in the head. The father's daughter was never idle. She could watch something once and then could do it. But, despite her hard work and uncomplaining nature, her stepmother and stepsister wanted to be rid of her.

The two of them came up with a plan. On a warm day, the two stepsisters were sent by their mother to spin by the well where it was a bit cooler. The mother gave her daughter flax to spin and gave her stepdaughter prickly nettle with bristles to spin. To pass the time, the mother's daughter proposed a spinning contest. Whoever's thread broke first had to climb down into the well. The father's daughter agreed because she was an excellent spinner, but the stinging nettle fibers itched her fingers and the bristles cut her thread.

Down she went into the well until she found herself, unharmed, in a meadow filled with flowers and tall grasses. Walking along, she came to a hedge with a nest of blue birds. She was about to climb over the hedgerow when it spoke to her.

"Please do not crush my branches or step hard on my leaves and I might be of use to you sometime," said the hedge.

The girl carefully jumped over the bushes without touching a leaf or disturbing the nest. Three little blue birds followed her. Soon, she came to a spotted cow with a bucket hanging from her left horn. Her udder was painfully full and stretched out with milk.

"Would you be so kind as to milk me?" pleaded the cow. "I am so full; it hurts. You may drink as much milk as you like and then please throw the rest over my hooves. Someday, I will gladly repay the favor."

As soon as the girl set the pail at the udder and touched it, the milk flowed. She drank her fill and then poured the rest over the cow's hooves. As requested, she returned the pail to the cow's horn.

A bit farther, the girl came to a large sheep whose wool was so thick and long that it dragged on the ground. A pair of shears hung from one of his horns.

"Won't you please help me?" he said. "My wool is choking me and catching on everything. Please cut it off. Take what you will and wrap the rest around my neck. Perhaps someday I may help you."

She did as he asked and was on her way when she came to an apple tree with bowed branches loaded with ripe, red apples. The tree begged her to carefully pick all the apples, eat her fill, and then stack the rest at the foot of the tree and someday the tree would help her. The girl did so, and after stacking the last of the apples, she walked on munching an apple.

After walking a long way, she came to the house of a troll and her daughter. The girl asked if she could work there, but the wrinkled little troll shook her head.

"We've never had a maid who could do the work properly," she complained.

"Please give me a chance," the girl begged. "If you don't like my service, then you don't have to pay me. Just give me a week to show you."

The old troll raised her eyebrow and grinned, "So be it. Take this sieve and bring it back full of water."

Taking the sieve to the well, the girl wondered how a sieve could carry water. The three birds who had followed her now sang out, "Cover it with clay, stuff it with straw, and then the water will stay."

When she returned with water, the mother troll made a face sour as vinegar. To try the girl, the troll gave her yet another difficult task.

"Clean out the barn and milk the cows," she screamed.

The large pitchfork was so heavy the girl could barely move it.

Chirping, the birds sang out, "Use the broom to clean the room."

As she swept, the dirt and dung flew out the barn until it was spotless. The cows were stubborn, kicking and moving about as the girl tried to milk them.

The little birds sang, "Give us our fill and the cows will be still."

The girl managed to squeeze a few drops of milk for the birds and suddenly, the cows behaved. She brought a pail of frothy, warm milk to the old hag troll.

"Someone is helping you!" said the hag, stamping her foot in anger. "Well then, take this black wool and wash it until it is white!"

Frowning, the girl took the wool to the washing tub by the well. The little birds sang, "Dip it in the water but do not rub and it will come out white from the tub."

To her delight, the clean wool looked like white fluffy clouds, but the crabby troll scowled.

"You can do everything, so you are no good to me," the old hag snarled, for she planned to eat the girl if she failed to do these chores.

"For your wages, you may choose one of these boxes," said the hag.

Before the girl, she placed three boxes; one red, the second one green, and the third, blue. The blue birds sang, "It is true, to be safe, choose the blue."

The girl took the little blue box. The old hag screamed in surprise, "Oh, you had to pick THAT one, didn't you!"

Picking up a hot iron from the fireplace, the troll swung it at the girl who turned and ran down the lane to the apple tree. The troll and her daughter chased after the girl to get the blue treasure box back but the apple tree hid the girl under its branches.

Catching her breath, the old troll called out to the apple tree, "Have you seen a maiden running by?"

"Oh yes, she is long gone," the tree replied. "You will never catch up to her."

The old hag and her daughter were tired and started back home. When it was safe, the tree lifted its branches. The girl thanked the apple tree and ran on. Soon, she heard the old hag and her daughter clattering behind her.

The sheep called out to the girl, "This way, hide under my wool or else they will tear you to bits."

Panting, the old hag came up to the sheep, "Have you seen a maiden pass by?"

"Hmm, it was about an hour ago I saw her," the sheep replied. "She must be far away by now."

The weary hag and her daughter decided to head back home. Thanking the sheep, the girl pushed on until she saw the cow. The old troll and her daughter changed their minds and again were tracking the girl. The cow told her to hide under her udder.

The cranky old hag cried out to the cow, "Have you seen a maiden running by?"

"I saw a girl running so fast that she must be far, far away by now," replied the cow.

The trolls groaned and trudged toward home.

The girl was finally near the hedgerow. But the old hag and her daughter once again came in hot pursuit. Hiding the girl under its twigs and leaves, the hedgerow spread out to make it difficult to cross.

"Have you seen a maiden pass by?" the tired troll screamed out.

"No, I have not," replied the hedge as it grew taller and wider.

This time, the troll and her daughter gave up and went all the way home. The girl thanked the hedge and found her way back home. Her stepmother was furious and sent the father's daughter out to live in the pigsty. The girl scrubbed it clean. When she was settled, she opened the blue box. Out of the box came gold and silver ornaments that decorated her walls. All manner of lovely things made her pigsty look like a palace fit for a grand king. When the mother and her stepsister saw this, they demanded an explanation. The girl told them of the troll's house at the bottom of the well and that the treasure box was payment for her labor.

The mother's daughter wanted a box with gold and silver too. So she jumped down the well and found herself in the meadow. As she walked, she came along the hedgerow but tramped her way through, cracking the twigs and ignoring the hedge's request. She milked the cow, but after drinking some she tossed the rest on the ground. She did not bother to shear the wooly sheep, and when she came to the overloaded apple tree, she picked an apple and left the rest on the bending branches. Off she went to the farmhouse where the troll and her daughter lived.

The stepsister asked for work but the old hag didn't want lazy girls or girls who were too clever and cheated her. But the stepsister insisted.

"I will give you a chance," the old hag said. "Go fetch water in this sieve."

At the well, the stepsister tried again and again to collect water but it simply poured out of the sieve. The little birds sang, "Cover it with clay, stuff it with straw, then the water will stay."

Annoyed, the stepsister would not listen to the chirping birds and pitched pebbles at them until they flew away. With the empty sieve, she returned to the house only to be scolded and sent out to clean the barn and milk the cow. But the stepsister could not lift the pitchfork and the cows kicked her. When she returned with no milk and the barn work not done, the old troll punished her and then sent her out to wash the black wool until it gleamed white.

The stepsister returned with the wool still as black as coal. The old hag just wanted to be rid of the useless, complaining girl so she offered her three boxes from which to choose; a red box, a green box, or a blue box. The stepsister chose the red box because it was the biggest and the brightest. The old troll smirked and the stepsister found her way home without any trouble.

Excitement seized the daughter and her mother as they headed to the large barn, dreaming the red box would fill the big room with lovely things. They opened the box. Out poured writhing snakes, warty toads, and stinging insects, but worse yet, whenever the mother's daughter opened her mouth, worms and cockroaches crawled out along with other nasty things. That was how the old hag paid the lazy girl for her efforts.

Notes

Trolls are magical, mythological beings who prefer to live in isolated areas and are generally unfriendly to humans. The Norwegian variety of trolls is inclined to be cannibalistic. They can be giant in size or dwarf sized. They are often characterized as ugly and stupid but also strong and brutal. Trolls sometimes steal humans and keep them as slaves. Trolls like to look at shiny objects like gold, silver, and jewels. In this story, the troll is more like the witch, Baba Yaga, a Slavic supernatural being.

—KB

The Raja's Son and Princess Labam

A folktale from India

Once there was and once there was not, a raja whose only son loved to hunt. The young man's mother, the rani, told the prince that hunting was allowed in the north, the east, or the west of the land, but he was not to go south. She feared the prophecy in which her son would learn of Princess Labam and leave his home and parents to find her.

Many a day the young prince would hunt in the three permitted directions. But the time came when he grew bored. His curiosity led him to the southern jungle, where bright green, blue, and red parrots flocked in great numbers. The raja's son shot at the parrots, scattering the birds in a cloud of colors and complaining voices. All but one, that is. The large majestic parrot, Raja Hiraman, remained and called to the other parrots.

"Do not leave or I will tell Princess Labam."

With his eyes wide in surprise, the prince said, "You can speak! Please tell me who is Princess Labam and where does she dwell?"

"Princess Labam is beautiful beyond measure, but you will never find her," said the angry Hiraman and flew away.

With his head down, the prince lumbered home thinking of the mysterious Princess Labam. Slumped in his bed, he would not speak or eat, and as time passed, he grew weaker.

At last, he could stand it no more and announced to his mother and father, "I cannot live in peace until I meet Princess Labam. Where is her country? I must go to her."

"We do not know where she lives," said the raja. "We only know that the journey will be dangerous. You are our only son and we are begging you not to go, for we fear you may never return."

"I cannot eat. I cannot sleep. I must try and find her. If I am successful, I will return to you. But danger or not, I must go!" exclaimed the prince.

With a heavy heart, the raja gave his only son a fine horse and a sack filled with rupee coins. The prince gathered up his weapons and all he would need for his journey. With tears in her eyes, the rani gave him her saffron-yellow handkerchief filled with candied dates.

Thus ready for his journey, the prince mounted his white horse and rode into the jungle. He traveled to a clear pond where he refreshed himself and his horse. Opening his mother's silk handkerchief, he took out a sweet only to find that this date and all of his dates were covered with ants. Even though he was hungry and tired, the prince put the sweets on the ground and let the ants feast.

Impressed by this deed, the king of the ants said, "Thank you for your kindness and for sharing your food. If you ever need help, just think of us and we will attend to you."

Smiling, the prince thanked the ant raja and continued on his quest. As he entered another jungle, thick with vines and trees, a roar of pain filled the air. There, in a clearing, the prince saw a tiger crouched, chewing his paw.

"What is the matter?" the prince asked.

Mournfully, the tiger answered, "I have a thorn in my paw that has bothered me for twelve days."

"If you promise not to eat me," said the prince, "I will help you."

"I will not eat you if you take out this thorn," cried the tiger.

With his knife, the prince quickly cut out the sharp, long thorn and wrapped the paw in his yellow silk handkerchief. The tiger howled in pain and his wife heard him. From across the jungle the tigress raced to her husband as the frightened prince jumped behind a tree. When the tiger told his wife that the raja's son had cured his aching paw, she also agreed not eat him.

The tiger said, "Raja's son, if you ever need help, think of us and we will come to your aid."

The prince spent the night with the tigers and the next day set out again on his journey. As he rode through the third jungle, he heard a loud argument. Four monks shouted, "I want this" and "This was meant for me."

The four fakirs were quarreling over the belongings of their dead teacher. Dismounting his horse, the prince asked about the argument. The men explained the value of the four items left by their master: The bed would magically take its owner where ever the owner wished to go; the bag gave whatever its owner requested, be it food, jewels, or clothing; the stone bowl provided as much clean cool water as its owner wanted; and finally a stick and rope would defend their owner by beating and tying up any enemy.

"I think I can help you resolve this problem," said the prince. "I will shoot four arrows in four directions. The first to bring me an arrow will be the first to choose the item he wants most."

The fakirs agreed and the prince rapidly shot four arrows in the four cardinal directions. Running in different directions, the monks scattered. Quickly, the prince gathered up the bowl, bag, rope, and stick and then sat on the bed and said,

"Take me to the country of Princess Labam."

The bed rose into the air and flew over oceans, mountains, and forests before settling softly on the ground. With his treasures, the prince walked until he came to the home of an old woman.

"Auntie, what country is this?" he asked.

"It is the country of Princess Labam," she replied. "Where are you from?"

"I come from a far way land and I am very tired. May I spend the night here with you?" the prince inquired.

"You must not," she said. "The king forbids strangers to stay in his country. I cannot let you spend the night in my home."

"But I have no place to go and the jungle beasts might eat me. Please, help me. It is growing dark," pleaded the handsome prince.

The old woman softened, "You may spend just this night. If the king discovers that you stayed here, he will cast me into prison."

As she began to prepare dinner, the prince stopped her.

He took out the bag and commanded, "Bag, give us dinner fit for a king."

Instantly, two golden plates appeared, filled with savory foods and juicy fruits. Then, with his stone bowl, the prince summoned sweet, clear water. The old woman was in awe and knew that the raja's son was indeed a special young man. Together, the old woman and the prince ate with great pleasure.

As darkness surrounded them, the prince asked," Auntie, why do you not light a lamp?"

"I have no need," she replied, "for Princess Labam will soon sit on the palace roof and light up the town like day with her brilliance and beauty."

Before long, the princess, dressed in her finest jewels and a diamond crown, appeared on the roof. Only at night did the princess come out of her tower, but when she did, her radiance shed light throughout the land. The raja's son was lovestruck. Truly the princess was the most beautiful woman he had ever seen. He gazed at her until midnight, when she returned to her room. Everyone went to sleep, but the prince.

He sat on his magic bed and said, "Take me to Princess Labam's bedroom."

The bed floated into the window of the princess's room where she lay sleeping. Her skin was smooth; her lips full and red. The prince stood, admiring at her for a while, and then took out his magical bag and demanded a large quantity of betel leaves to set on her night table as a gift of respect and introduction. Returning to the old woman's home, he slept peacefully.

The next morning, the princess woke up to find her servant chewing a betel leaf. No one knew who had brought the leaves. The princess frowned.

That same morning, the old woman asked the prince to leave. But he complained of a headache and begged her to let him stay until he was well. She agreed so long as he stays hidden inside her house.

Night fell and the princess again illuminated the darkness until midnight. Everyone went to bed except the prince, who flew again to her bedroom. Gently, he draped a delicate shawl, laced with pearls, over the sleeping princess. Smiling, he returned to the old woman's house.

The next day, the princess exclaimed to her mother, "Look what the god Khuda has given me!" She wrapped the lovely shawl around her shoulders and danced about her room. Her mother smiled, but still wondered who might have brought the gift.

After midnight, the prince once more flew to the princess's bedroom. This time he had a delicate golden ring for her. He carefully slid the ring onto her finger. Startled, she woke up.

"Who are you?" she gasped. "How did you get here?"

"Please do not be frightened. I am the son of a great raja," he replied. "Hiraman parrot told me of you. I have left my family and home far away to find you. I wish to marry you."

She looked into his golden brown eyes and his fine face. Indeed, with his rich clothing and manners, he must be a raja's son.

"You appear to be as you say," she said. "I will not have you hung, but will tell my parents that I wish to marry you."

The next morning the princess told her father of the raja's son and of her wish to marry him. The king always required his daughter's suitors to perform tasks. If the suitor failed to do as the king bid, he was put to death. The old woman warned the prince, but the prince would not leave.

In the royal courthouse, the prince stood before the king. His first task was to crush the oil out of eighty pounds of mustard seeds in one day. If the raja's son did not succeed, death would be his reward. The prince shook his head in despair, but he took the seeds to the old woman's home to try. There he saw an ant and remembered the ant raja's promise. As soon as he thought of the ants, they appeared and began to work. They worked through the night as the prince lay sleeping. Finally every last mustard seed had been crushed and the oil removed.

The next morning the prince awoke and was filled with gratitude. He thanked his tiny friends and then took the oil and the spent seeds to the king.

Amazed and angered, the king said, "You may not marry my daughter until you have completed the next task. You must fight two demons and kill them."

The prince was taken to a cage were two fearsome, man-eating demons were kept. The king had locked them up because he did not know how to kill them. All other suitors had perished in their attempts to slay the hideous creatures.

The prince looked at the bloodthirsty demons and thought of the tigers. Suddenly, the tigers were by his side. A gruesome battle soon took place with screams and roars, teeth slashing, claws tearing, and fur flying everywhere. The tigers pinned the demons to the ground and the prince released his magic rope to tie them up. Then, with his sword, he chopped the demons' heads off. The prince bowed to the tigers and then brought the heads to the king.

"Ah," said the king, awed but secretly feeling grateful. "There is a third task you must do before I give you my daughter's hand in marriage. In the clouds, there is a kettledrum. You must go into the sky and beat the drum four times. If you do not do this, I will have to kill you."

Sitting on his enchanted bed, the prince flew into the sky and beat the kettledrum. Dumbfounded, the king looked up into the sky and heard the drumbeats. Still, the king did not want to give his precious daughter to the raja's son. He thought of yet another seemingly impossible task.

When the prince returned, the king said, "You have surprised me and have completed all but the final task. Tomorrow I will give you a wax hatchet. With it, you must chop through this mighty Banyan tree. If you fail, you die."

After midnight, the unhappy prince flew on his magic bed to the princess's bedroom. With downcast eyes he told her of the insurmountable task. She smiled.

"Do not despair," she said. "Do as I say and you will succeed."

Princess Labam plucked a long shiny black hair from her head and gave it to the raja's son. She told him to whisper to the Banyan tree, "Princess Labam orders you to allow this hair to cut you in half."

The prince stretched the hair along the edge of the hatchet's wax blade as the princess had instructed him. As the hair touched the tree, it split in two. At long last, the king granted the prince his daughter's hand in marriage.

A great celebration was arranged with all the rajas and kings from surrounding countries attending the wedding. As a parting wedding gift, the princess's father gave camels, horses, servants, and money to the happy couple. The prince's parents marveled at the story of his journey and rejoiced to have him home again. As years passed, they all lived in peace and contentment, and the prince always kept the enchanted bed, bag, bowl, rope, and stick nearby.

Notes

The betel leaf, when chewed, acts as a mild stimulant, similar to nicotine. They have a peppery taste and with regular use, stain the teeth a reddish-brown. They are popular in Asian countries and are often offered to strangers to ease awkward social introductions.

Ants are amazing creatures whose colonies behave like one huge organism and are noted for their hard-working behavior. There are over 12,000 species of ants. They communicate through chemical signals called pheromones. The pheromones can act as a mating call by the queen ants or as an alarm to warn of danger to the colony. Some species of ants cultivate fungi for food, while others raise aphids for the honeydew they produce.

—KB

General Dog and His Army

A Croatian folktale

It was a long time ago, before your grandmother's grandmother was born, that there lived in the hills of Croatia a young man named Branko. There had been a time when his family was wealthy and powerful but slowly bad luck had crept into their castle. Soon death took his parents, fear took his servants, and a lack of money took his friends, and he was left all alone. All that was left to his name, besides his run-down castle, was his trusty musket, his loyal horse, and his faithful dog. Though he needed his horse and musket when hunting for his food, it was his dog that was his true friend. At night the dog guarded the castle, and during the day he never left Branko's side. Often Branko would talk to his dog as they walked the forest or sat under a tree and ate their lunch. Branko knew that his dog understood every word his master spoke.

One day Branko left the horse tied to a tree and went with his dog into the woods to hunt. When they were out of sight, a fox walked up to the horse and said, "You are well fed and well cared for, my friend. You must have a good master."

"Indeed, I do," replied the horse.

"Well, I am tired of living paw to mouth and often going hungry. I will just wait here and keep you company and meet this master of yours. Perhaps he will take me into his service." The fox curled up by the horse and waited.

Soon Branko and his dog returned from the woods. When Branko saw the fox, he raised his musket to his shoulder. He was just about to shoot when the fox spoke.

"Young master, don't shoot. I am looking for a home and, after seeing how well cared for your horse is, I wanted to offer myself to you as a servant. I can take care of your horse and clean your stable. I can also help guard your home at night."

Branko knew he had no servants and thought the fox seemed very sincere, so he lowered his gun. "We can try it, but my dog runs the castle and every thing in it," he said. "So you must obey him and follow his orders."

The fox agreed, and they all went back to the castle. In no time the dog found that the fox was a willing and faithful servant. Sometime later they all went hunting and, while Branko and the dog were in the woods, the fox stayed behind to guard the horse and keep him company. Not long after Branko left, a huge bear lumbered into the clearing and approached the horse and the fox.

"Don't you come any closer. This horse is under my protection," snarled the fox, standing between the horse and the bear, teeth bared.

"A horse under the protection of a fox? What nonsense is this?" asked the bear.

"My master treats me well, and this is his horse. My master's house is warm, and he feeds me well and takes care of me. Instead of threatening us, why not wait and join his service? Your days of wandering in search of food will be over. You will have a roof over your head and friends at your side."

The bear thought this might be a good idea, so he stretched himself out on the grass and was soon fast asleep next to the fox. When Branko returned and he saw the bear, he lifted his musket to his shoulder, but the fox moved in front of the bear and said, "Master, this bear wishes to be in your service."

Branko thought for a moment and replied, "I need a strong servant. You may come with us and live in the castle, but remember that my faithful dog is in charge. You must obey him." The bear agreed, and they all went back home together.

The bear proved to be just as loyal as the fox. As time passed, word soon spread throughout the woods that Branko was a good master. More and more animals came to his door to ask to be in his service. First came a wolf, then a mouse, then a mole, and a hare. Finally, the strangest creature in the forest came, the kumrekusha, a huge bird that could lift a horse off its feet and fly away with it. The kumrekusha was so strong that Branko could ride on her back as she soared through the air.

Soon, all the animals that lived in the castle had become great friends and were devoted to their kind master. One day, while the dog and his friends were talking, he said, "Do we not have the best master in the world?"

They all agreed.

"It seems to me that he is lonely," said the dog. "I think he needs a wife, but not any woman will do. She must be the fairest lady in all the land, beautiful and kind."

The little mouse said, "The fairest lady in all the land is the king's daughter. I have seen her with my own eyes." The little mouse had visited many houses and seen many things. "But, she is locked up in a tall tower surrounded by a strong wall and many guards. How could we get her here?"

The fox had an idea. "The kumrekusha can do it. She can fly over the wall, and I will help her. I will drop off her back into the garden and change myself into a kitten. No one can resist a baby animal. When the princess comes down to play with me, our great friend can swoop down and carry her away." The animals agreed that it was a splendid idea.

So, the fox was dropped into the garden and changed himself into a kitten. When the princess saw the precious little cat chasing a butterfly, she instantly ran down into the garden to play with it. The kumrekusha swept down, picked up both the princess and the fox, and flew home while the guards helplessly stood by. Instead of being afraid, the princess was thrilled by the adventure.

When she arrived at Branko's castle, the princess was amazed to see all these animals living in harmony with each other. When she saw Branko, she knew that the kind young man must be her husband. When Branko saw the wonder in her face, and no fear of the animal servants that surrounded her, he knew that she must be his wife.

Plans were quickly made, and the wedding took place. All the creatures of the woods attended as honored guests. The princess took easily to the ways of the castle, and soon the animals loved her as much as they loved Branko.

But, the princess's father was angry that a bird and a cat had kidnapped his daughter. Word was sent across the land that there was a reward for news of her whereabouts. Soon, an old beggar came and told the king that his daughter was married to a penniless young noble named Branko and lived with him in his castle, protected by the animals that served him. The king gave the old man a bag of gold and sent him on his way.

The next day, the king's army was assembled and began its march on Branko's castle.

When word came to the dog that the king was leading his army to take back his daughter, Branko's faithful servant assembled all the other animals.

"The king is coming to take our dear mistress away and punish our master. We need a great army to fight them. Who will fight with us to protect those who have shown us so much kindness?"

The bear rose to his full height and said, "My kin will fight. I will bring a hundred bears to the field of battle."

The fox quickly added, "I can bring two hundred foxes."

The wolf snarled, "I can bring three hundred wolves."

The hare, mole, and mouse spoke up. "And I can bring four hundred hares. And I can bring six hundred moles. And I can bring a thousand mice."

"There are only fifty kumrekushas in the whole world," said the great bird, "but all of us will be there."

"And I," said the dog, "will lead the army and be your general. Now go and call your kinsmen here and be quick about it."

When the army was assembled, it truly was an impressive sight to see— thousands of animals, ready to fight for Branko and his lady.

General Dog gave his first orders. "Tonight, when the king's army settles to sleep, I want the wolves and bears to fall upon their horses. This will force the king to send for more horses. On the next night, I want the mice to gnaw through the leather straps of the bridles and reins. This time the army will have to send for more bridles and reins or stop to repair the damaged ones. The next night, I want the foxes and hares to gnaw through the ropes that hold the tents up and the ones that pull the cannons and supply wagons. These tactics will delay the army as it marches on our home."

When the king and his men awoke the next day, all of their horses were dead. The king had to send men on foot to get more horses. The next day they awoke to find all of the bridles and reins gnawed in half and spent all day repairing them. The next day after that they awoke as all the tents fell down around them and all the cannons sat with worthless ropes. So, they spent an entire day repairing ropes.

By the time more horses could arrive, the king's army had begun to fear the army of animals. All of the king's soldiers were constantly looking over their shoulders to see what might happen next. Finally, all the bridles and reins were mended, the cannon ropes rebraided, and the army ready to march again. Now, it was time for the moles to do their work.

All night long they dug deep into the earth to make traps for the king's men and their horses. The bears and wolves carried away the dirt so no sign of the moles' work was visible. The next day the king's army awoke and there were no animals in sight.

"The cowardly animals have deserted their master," declared the king. "Now we will march on Branko's castle and take back what is mine," he cried.

But no sooner did the army begin to march that they also began to fall into the deep traps dug by the moles. As they struggled to get up out of the earth, the sky was darkened by the flight of the kumrekushas as they dropped huge rocks down on the heads of the soldiers.

The king cried out in despair. "We cannot fight Branko. The animals of the earth and the birds of the sky are all against us." Defeated, he and his army returned to his own kingdom.

Not long afterward, because of the kindness of Branko, the king was reconciled with his daughter and her prince, and they all lived in peace and harmony, just like the animals that served in Branko's castle. And there always was a place of honor for General Dog.

Notes

Dogs were domesticated about 15,000 years ago. The average dog has a sense of smell that is tens of thousands of times more sensitive than a human. Dogs use their sense of smell in search and rescue missions to help find people in the rubble of buildings after natural disasters like hurricanes or earthquakes. Today many dogs are used to aid the visually impaired and also people who are prone to seizures. Scientists have discovered that dogs can actually detect a seizure before it happens and warn their human companion. In fact, scientists predict that someday soon dogs will be trained to detect cancer cells before anyone knows they are present.

—DK

Section 5

Creatures of the Imagination

The Boy Who Drew Cats

A folktale from Japan

A long time ago, or so the old people say, there lived a boy named Tomo. His father and mother worked long hours in the rice fields alongside his older brothers and sisters. They were big and strong, but Tomo was small and he often watched the farm cats instead of weeding the vegetable patch. Ever since he was able to walk, Tomo followed the farm cats, watching, watching, watching. He giggled when they played with string but was fascinated when they pounced on a mouse or sharpened their claws on a tree or fence post. Tomo loved cats.

He not only thought of cats and watched cats, he even dreamt of cats. Soon, he began to draw graceful cat figures in the dirt with a stick. He drew all sorts of cats: sleeping cats with curled up tails, cats stalking in the tall grass, hissing cats with arched backs, playful cats wrestling in the weeds. One day his parents found him with their oldest son's brush and ink pot. Tomo had painted cats on the floor, the wall, his kimono, and on a few bits of rice paper. His parents were in despair. What were they going to do with him? It was hard enough to feed their large family, and although he had grown, Tomo was not strong enough to work in the fields. He was a good son and a clever boy but he was not fit to be a farmer. His grandfather suggested that they take him to the temple to become a Kozō, a boy studying for priesthood.

A priest wearing a saffron-yellow robe asked Tomo many questions and Tomo answered thoughtfully and with respect. His clever answers pleased the priest, so he accepted Tomo into the temple school. Tomo was delighted to have his own brushes and ink paste. He dutifully learned to form the Japanese characters with the fine point of his brush. He studied hard but still drew cats where ever he found an empty space, on the corners of his lesson papers, on his arms, on his desk, on his sleeping mat. When his teachers scolded him, he tried to stop, but before long an image of a cat would come to him and he just had to call it into being with fluid lines of black ink on white paper. The good priests of Buddha's temple finally lost patience. They told Tomo that he was meant to be an artist and no longer had a place as a student in the temple school. As he prepared to leave, a kindly old priest came to say good-bye. He gave Tomo rice balls with this advice.

"On your way back home, remember to avoid large open places at night. Find a small place to sleep."

Tomo stepped out the temple gate but was too ashamed to go home. His parents would be disappointed and embarrassed by his failure. Instead of heading back to his village, he struck out toward a town with another temple. Perhaps these priests would take him as a Kozo,

"If I am given another chance," he vowed, "I will work very hard to please my teachers and not disgrace my family."

It was almost dusk when Tomo spotted the temple on the rise of a white-capped mountain above the town. As he approached the entrance, he saw a light glimmer inside. The light was to lure innocent travelers to the temple haunted by a rat goblin.

Unaware of the danger, Tomo knocked and knocked. The sounds seemed to echo in the temple. The door was unlocked so Tomo called inside, "Konbanwa, hello, is anyone here?"

His voice sounded hollow in the great hall. Silence answered and Tomo thought maybe the priests were in prayer. He set down his bundle on the dusty floor and sat beside it to rest. Still, no one came. Then he spied a broom standing in the corner.

"Surely the priests would welcome an industrious boy who cleaned their floors!" Tomo thought. So he began to sweep the floor and knock down the cobwebs in his path.

When he was done, he looked at the spotless white floors and imagined cats. He took out his brushes and ink paste and began to draw cats—large cats, small cats, crouching cats, cats in midair, cats playing, cats fighting. He saw paper folding screens that divided off the great hall and smiled. Soon they were filled with lively figures of cats—brawling cats, sitting cats, stalking cats with sharp claws, and sleeping cats curled in a ball.

Before long, Tomo's eyelids grew heavy. He yawned as he unrolled his sleeping mat in the middle of the great hall. But as he lay down, something felt wrong. He remembered the old priest's words, "Find a small place to sleep." Behind a folding screen he found an empty cabinet that smelled of incense. It was just big enough for him and his bundle. Inside, he slid the cabinet door shut and fell asleep.

In the dead of the night, he woke to the sound of a loud crash. Fierce growling, snarling, and hissing sounds pierced the air. Tomo clutched his bundle and trembled with fear. It was as if monsters were battling in the temple hall. The bloodcurdling screams continued as wood smashed and heavy bodies shook the floor. Finally the noise ended, but Tomo could not move.

He waited until he saw the bright morning light through a crack in the cabinet door. Then he quietly slid the door open and peeped out. The paper screen shielded his view of the great hall, so he crawled over to peer around the screen. A small cry escaped his lips.

There, in the middle of the temple hall floor, lay a rat goblin in a pool of black blood. The evil creature was the size of a water buffalo and had long sharp teeth and claws. Who could have defeated such an awesome foe? Turning, Tomo looked at the temple folding screen and saw that all of his cat figures now had blood dripping from their fangs and claws. They had saved him. With his heart full of gratitude, Tomo bowed low to his cat drawings.

He climbed up the tower to the temple bell to summon the priests. When the townspeople heard the bell pealing, they hurried to the deserted temple and were amazed to see the dead rat goblin. Many a warrior had attempted to destroy the monstrous rat but failed. Now, the priests could return to the temple and the townspeople no longer feared that their crops would be eaten by the giant rat. They rewarded Tomo with a purse of gold and silver coins.

Tomo did not become a priest. Instead, he went to Kyoto, the Emperor's city, to pursue his studies in art. He became a famous artist whose fluid lines were said to be like music on paper. His drawings of cats seemed so real that one could imagine them leaping right off the parchment.

Notes

This story was also known as "The Picture-Cats and the Rat" in the Japanese regions of Chugoku and Shikoku. In that version, the main character, the boy, later becomes the abbot of the temple. In Lafcadio Hearn's version, the boy grows up to become a famous artist. Hearn embroidered the tale further by haunting the temple with a rat goblin.

Cats are considered good luck in Japanese culture. They represent prosperity and success. You may have seen a little golden figurine of a cat waving with its left front paw and holding a coin with the other paw. It is the Japanese Fortune Cat, Maneki Neko, and is a cultural icon.

Cats originated in Africa, descending from wildcats such as lions, tigers and cougars. Some believe that cats were first domesticated in ancient Egypt. Cats are the most popular pet in the world and in the United States there are about 75 million cats. They eat the equivalent of five mice a day and kill billions of birds and somewhere around five billion rodents a year.

—KB

The Seal Hunter and the Merman

A folktale from Scotland

Once there lived a man in the north of Scotland who made his living by hunting seals and selling their fur. He was able to make a good living because the seals came to lie on the rocks along the shore, near his cottage, and slept there in the warm sun.

Now many people in the village said that *selkies* were mingled among the seals. These creatures—mermen and mermaids—lived in a kingdom that lay deep on the sea's floor. The villagers said that you could always know the difference between the two creatures because the seafolk were larger than the seals. When the seal hunter heard these stories, though, he only laughed. "They are nothing more than old tales with not a thread of truth in them," he said.

Now, one day the hunter crept up on a huge seal that was dozing in the sun. Taking careful aim, he stabbed it with his long knife, but the creature reared up and dove into the water. Screaming, it swam away with the knife still stuck in its side.

The angry seal hunter couldn't believe what he saw. He should have killed the seal with one stroke; instead he had lost his best hunting knife. As he headed back to his cottage, he met a stranger on the path. The man was very tall and the horse he rode was huge. The hunter stopped and looked up at the man who, in turn, reined in his horse to ask the seal hunter about his occupation. Overjoyed with the hunter's answer, the stranger explained that he was in search of a large quantity of sealskins and must have them that very night.

The hunter replied that he couldn't possibly fill the man's order because he had just lost his only good hunting knife. Besides, the seals had left the shore and would not return until the next morning.

"I know a place where the seals linger all day long," replied the stranger. "Climb up behind me. I'll take you there and provide you with a good blade for the hunt."

The seal hunter agreed and soon he and the stranger were galloping away. They rode like the wind until they came to a cliff that overlooked the sea. Looking down the seal hunter saw no rocks; he saw no seals. Just as he was about to speak, he felt the horse crouch and the horseman, the horse, and he himself all plunged over the side of the cliff and into the depths of the sea.

As they sank deeper and deeper, the hunter knew that he was facing certain death. Then he realized that he was still breathing. He looked to his side and there was the stranger and his horse, sinking as quickly through the water as they had ridden on land.

Finally, they came to the ocean's floor. There, they stood before a great gate made of coral and the white bones of huge sea creatures. The gate slowly opened by itself, and they entered into a great hall. The walls were lined with mother-of-pearl and the sandy floor was firm and shining yellow in the glow of some unseen light.

The hall was full, not with men, but with seals. When the hunter turned to his companion to ask him what this meant, he saw that the stranger too was now a seal. Then glancing into a nearby mirror, he saw what he could not believe. He also had turned into a beautiful seal, with sleek thick fur and black eyes. Utterly amazed, the hunter just stood there.

At first the seals ignored him, moving slowly and silently around the hall, their eyes full of sorrow. When they spoke, he heard only a low and mournful sound and often saw a tear run down their cheeks. Finally, they seemed to notice him and whisper to each other. His guide left and returned carrying a large knife.

"Have you seen this before?" he asked.

"Of course," the hunter replied. "That is the knife that I lost this morning." Then he realized that he must have been brought here because of his attack on the large seal. He fell to his knees and begged for forgiveness, expecting at any moment to be attacked.

Instead, the seals pressed in on him, rubbing their soft noses against his fur. They comforted the man and quietly assured him that violence was not in their nature. They asked him not to be afraid and said that he would not be harmed. They would always be his friends as long as he did what they asked of him.

"Tell me what it is, and I will do it."

His guide, the stranger who brought him to the hall, led him into another room. There they found a great brown seal lying on a bed of seaweed, a wound in his side.

"This is my father, our king," said the guide. "You wounded him this morning. You thought him to be a seal, but he is a *selkie*, a merman who understands your speech and reasons just as you do. Only the hands of the one who attacked him can heal him.

"I have no healing skills, but I will do the best I can," said the hunter. He washed the wound and spread a salve that the king's son gave him. The touch of his hands seemed to act like magic. Before long the wound healed, and a long thin scar appeared across the side of the great merman. He rose from his bed as if he never had been wounded.

The three joined the merfolk in the great hall where laughing and singing celebrated the healing of the king. Then, one by one the sealfolk came by to touch the hunter with their fins. Each touch seemed to express their gratitude. The hunter found his ability to heal the merman hard to believe but he was even more astonished by the kindness of the supportive merfolk. He knew that after watching them grieve and rejoice, sing and dance, he could never hunt seals again for fear of injuring one of these kind creatures.

"You may return to your family now," said his guide and the host of the merfolk, "but only under one condition."

"Whatever it is, I will agree," said the hunter.

"You must never hunt seals again."

"I have already agreed with that in my heart," said the man.

His guide led him from the great hall and, in one tremendous leap, they were standing on the cliff again. As the water dripped off their fur, they lost their seal skins and took on the shape of the seal hunter and the tall stranger. They mounted the stranger's horse and rode toward the hunter's cottage.

When they reached the gate to the hunter's cottage, the hunter held out his hand to bid farewell to the merman. As he did this, the merman put a large, heavy sack into the hunter's hand.

"Because you have made a bargain with us, we need to make a bargain with you. We cannot ask you to give up your way of life without making amends for that request. This should keep you and your family comfortable until the end of your days." With those words the merman and his horse disappeared.

When the hunter emptied the sack on the kitchen table, he found gold coins and jewels, enough to make him a wealthy man. He never went to the sea to hunt again, but sometimes he would walk to the shore to watch the seals. He would wave and then listen as a few of them, those larger than the others, would call out in their beautiful voices and lift a flipper as if to say "hello."

———————

Notes

In Scotland mermen and merwomen are called selkies *from the Scottish word* selch, *which means seal. The* selkies *often come ashore in their more human form and interact with those people who live near the sea. Many people on the islands that surround Scotland believe that they themselves are actually descended from* selkies.

—DK

The Dragons of Ha Long Bay

A legend from Vietnam

Long ago, across a great ocean, there was a young country called Vietnam. The country was shaped like a comma that hugged the southeast coast of Asia. To the north, there lay a bountiful bay colonized by boat people. They lived in floating villages and made their living harvesting the abundant fish, oysters, seaweed, and other sea life. They were content with their lives and always showed gratitude to the ruler of the heavens, the Jade Emperor.

But trouble brewed to the far north of the bay. A mighty enemy set sail to invade the Vietnamese land. The fleet of enemy ships found the mouth of the northern Vietnamese bay and saw the riches of the waters. They wanted the bay for their own and entered with the intent of destroying the boat people and their villages.

From the heavens, the Jade Emperor saw the fierce invaders and sent a family of four dragons down to earth to protect the defenseless boat people. The serpentine creatures descended to earth and circled the ships, whipping up the winds and ripping the sails. From their mouths, they spilled jade and emeralds that turned into numerous islands blocking the ships. With their talons they dropped pearls the size of cannon balls that tore through the ships' hulls, sinking the fleet. In chaos, the sailors and warriors jumped overboard only to drown in the churning sea.

After the battle, the dragon family discovered earth to be a beautiful place and decided to stay instead of returning to the heavens. They loved best the calm turquoise waters of the bay and the reverence of the boat people.

The dragon family lived on earth and at times took on a human form to help guide the people of the bay.

And so, the dragons and the boat people lived in peace for many, many years. It is said that, when the dragons died, their serpentine bodies became the islets, mountainous ridges, and protruding limestone rocks that grace the bay. Sometimes, in the early morning light, the fading gray mist reveals the speckled green rolling mountains and bare black rock jutting from the water like the pointed tail of a dragon. Then, one can almost see those ancient guardians, who long ago saved the Vietnamese people of Ha Long Bay.

A grief shared by many is half a grief. A joy shared is twice a joy.

—Vietnamese folk saying

Notes

In ancient Vietnamese, Ha Long translates to mean "descending dragon." Ha Long Bay is a UNESCO World Heritage site because of its unique beauty. A Vietnamese origin myth describes the marriage of the dragon (king) with the goddess (queen) and tells that their children are the ancestors of the Vietnamese people. In other words, the Vietnamese are descended from the revered dragon clan. Vietnam's national father is portrayed as a holy dragon.

In Asian cultures, dragons are benevolent and usually associated with water in the form of rain (for agriculture) or rivers. They are said to be wise and can assume the shape of humans to aid the people.

Vietnam (officially known as the Socialist Republic of Vietnam) is a coastal country located in Southeast Asia. Its neighbor to the north is China and to the west are Laos, Thailand, and Cambodia. To the east, Vietnam is bordered by the South China Sea. Vietnam is the world's largest producer of cashew nuts and black pepper as well as the second largest exporter of rice and coffee. It is fast growing its information technology and recently began to export oil.

—KB

The Leshi Cat

A Russian folktale

Far, far away in Russia, very long ago, there lived a boy named Dmitry who was the only son of a kind merchant and his wife. Dmitry was a handsome fellow and led a happy life until his father died. Fearing poverty and starvation, Dmitry's pretty mother soon remarried, but this husband was a wicked, selfish man who immediately plotted to be rid of Dmitry.

"It is our duty to make a man out of your son," he said. "We must send Dmitry overseas to the island he inherited from his father. There he can serve as governor and begin to build his future."

"So soon? Are you sure?" asked his worried mother, "Dmitry is barely a man."

"Trust me," the stepfather replied. "It is best that he learns while he is young. The people of the island will show more kindness toward a youth," he insisted, shifting his eyes away from her.

"Then he must go," sighed his mother with watery eyes.

Within days, Dmitry was taken by ship to the island and dropped off. But there were no people on this island to govern. In fact, there appeared to be no one at all on the island. Dmitry was the victim of a cruel trick. Thirsty and hungry, he walked searching for fresh spring water and wild berries. Suddenly, he heard a great rumbling ruckus coming from the edge of the forest. It sounded like the world was coming to an end. Screams, growls, and the thudding of heavy bodies shook the island. As Dmitry crept closer, he saw two amazing creatures savagely fighting. A fiery devil was struggling with a Leshi, a woodland spirit shaped like a man with the legs of a goat. He had pale skin and glittering emerald eyes with long, green grass and curling vines growing from his head and beard. The Leshi's claws flew wildly at the devil as its hot hands grabbed the Leshi's throat.

Spying Dmitry, the devil shouted, "Dmitry, the merchant's son, I will reward you with gold if you help me slay this pesky Leshi."

"No, Dmitry, the merchant's son, help ME and I will be your friend forever," yelled the Leshi.

Dmitry had no use for gold on this forsaken island, but he certainly could use a friend! So he swung his sword at the devil cutting a gash into its red hide. The devil shrieked, spun up counterclockwise into the air, and vanished.

The Leshi bent over gasping, to catch his breath. Then he stood up with a broad smile and said, "Many thanks to you, Dmitry, the merchant's son. I have battled with the devil in this forest for longer than I can remember. Finally, I can rest. For your reward, you must go to my *dedushka,* my grandfather, who lives down this path. Do not take the thirteen sacks of gold he offers but ask if you might have the silver mirror with thirteen knobs. When you turn those knobs, thirteen sailors will jump out to do your bidding. Whatever you wish will be done."

Dmitry hiked quickly to the *dedushka*'s house. There he found a little old man with sparkling green eyes who gave him the requested mirror. He was so pleased to be rid of the devil that he gave Dmitry thirteen sacks of gold as well. As soon as he thanked the old man, Dmitry took the magic mirror and turned the knobs.

Instantly, thirteen sailors sprang from the mirror and said in unison, "Dmitry, the merchant's son, what do you wish?"

"Build me a castle of marble and crystal," Dmitry replied, "So that I might live like a lord."

No sooner had Dmitry spoken those words than it was done. He had invisible servants to tend to him and he wore the finest linen and leather. Indeed, he was quite happy but only for a while. Soon, he grew tired of living alone. He had no one to joke with or tell stories, and no one to love. So, again, Dmitry took the mirror and turned the knobs.

Instantly thirteen sailors sprang from the mirror, "Dmitry, the merchant's son, what do you wish?"

"Please bring me portraits of the loveliest maidens in the world," he said.

No sooner had the words left his mouth than the hall was decorated with pictures of fair maidens. Dmitry studied each one until he came to the daughter of the Emperor of China. As he looked into her kind eyes, he knew she was the one he loved the most. He took the mirror and turned the knobs. Instantly, the thirteen sailors sprang from the mirror.

"Please bring me the daughter of the Emperor of China," Dmitry ordered.

The sailors found the emperor's daughter locked up in a tall tower behind thick, sturdy doors. Until her father found her a husband to his liking, she was to remain in her prison chamber. She was lonely, but brave in her solitude. The princess slept soundly as the sailors gently lifted her bed. They carried her as fast as the wind to Dmitry's palace.

Dmitry looked at the face of the sweet, sleeping princess. Ebony black hair framed her peaceful face and silky, soft skin. He could not help himself. He leaned over to kiss the peach-blossom lips of the woman he loved. The princess woke up and screamed.

"Who are you and where am I?" she asked, her eyes wide as she looked wildly about the room.

"I am Dmitry and I have rescued you from your prison in the tower," Dmitry said gently.

The princess gazed at Dmitry and saw that his face was as kind and gentle as his voice. So many times while locked up in the tower she had wished for a friend. Now her dream of someone to love had come true.

Soon, the two were married and lived happily in their island palace. But the Emperor of China was furious. No one knew how the princess escaped from the locked, heavy doors in a tower 300 feet high. It was impossible. The emperor cursed and raged for days.

It so happened that in the emperor's court there lived an old grandmother, who knew the ancient ways of sorcery. She stared into her magic bowl filled with rain water collected at the full moon. There she saw the island where the princess now lived.

She went to the emperor and said, "I can return your daughter to the palace if you provide me with a fast ship."

The emperor knew of the grandmother's skills and granted her request. Under the old woman's direction, a fleet ship set off to the island and left her ashore. The old woman walked to the crystal palace and claimed to have been shipwrecked. Believing her story, the kind-hearted Dmitry gladly took her in.

The old woman quickly made herself a companion to the princess. Before long, the sorceress learned the secret of the magic mirror and its thirteen knobs.

"What fun it would be to order the sailors around," the old woman said. "Won't Dmitry share his toy with you?"

"Of course, Dmitry would give me anything I want," the princess replied with a toss of her head.

"Ah, then show me. Show me how much Dmitry loves you," said the cunning sorceress.

The princess only had to ask and Dmitry, who adored his wife, gladly gave her the mirror. The next day, while Dmitry was out hunting, the princess showed the mirror to the old woman. Quickly, the sorceress snatched it and turned the knobs.

Instantly the thirteen sailors appeared, "What do you command, old one?"

The witch replied, "Take the princess and me to the palace of the Emperor of China. Then destroy this island castle and leave Dmitry on a rock in the middle of the sea."

The princess screamed, but the sound caught in her throat as she whirled through the air, held tight by invisible hands until she landed back in the prison tower. At the same time, Dmitry clung to a rock as waves washed up around him. His fine castle was in ruins, but all was not lost.

Swimming toward him, the Leshi called out, "I have come to rescue you as you rescued me. Then my debt to you will be fully paid."

Soon, Dmitry and the Leshi, disguised as a big gray cat, found themselves on a ship headed for China. The ship's captain was only too happy to have Dmitry earn his keep as the cook, but in truth, it was the Leshi cat who did the work. When the cargo ship reached the shores of China, the captain bragged loudly of Dmitry's skills as a cook. Once the news of this cook reached the emperor, he demanded Dmitry serve him.

The old woman recognized Dmitry at once. She thought to banish him again to a rock in the middle of the ocean but was frightened of the big gray cat. Sensing its magical powers, she decided to wait until morning. Then she would use the mirror that she kept on a string around her throat.

The clever Leshi cat stalked the palace looking for a rat. He found one in the cellar and pounced on it.

"I will spare your life if you do something for me," the Leshi cat growled.

"Anything you ask!" squeaked the black rat.

"Go to the old woman's bed as she sleeps and chew the string around her neck. Then bring me the mirror," the Leshi cat commanded.

The rat skittered off and found the old woman snoring. Quickly, he chewed through the braided string and secured the silver mirror with his long teeth and then ran to the cat. The Leshi cat turned the mirror knobs and there stood the sailors.

"Carry the sleeping Dmitry and the princess back to their island," he commanded. "Rebuild the castle better than before and cast the old woman on a rock in the middle of the shark-infested sea."

When Dmitry and his bride woke up, they hugged and cried tears of joy. The Leshi's emerald eyes flashed a brilliant green as he declared, "Dmitry, my debt to you is paid. But if you lose the mirror again, you are on your own!"

Dmitry said, "Oh, dear Leshi, you have proven to be a true friend. I promise never to lose the mirror again."

Dmitry took the magic mirror and turned the wooden knobs. He ordered the sailors to bring good, honest people to settle nearby and farm the island.

"Let our island become a paradise where my wife and I will rule as queen and king."

And so it was done. The island became a place where people lived in happiness. The Leshi became Dmitry's trusted advisor and guided him with unfailing wisdom.

Notes

Leshies are nature spirits in Slavic mythology and have magical powers like fairies. They can shape-shift into other creatures or take on a human form and are often in the company of wolves or bears. The forest is the domain of the Leshi where it acts as protector or guardian of the animals and woodland. It is very territorial and often plays tricks on humans who trespass onto its land but sometimes can enter into an agreement with a human that is beneficial to both.

—KB

Damian and the Dragon

A folktale from Greece

There once was a king who had three sons and one daughter. One day, the king asked his sons to try and remember their dreams and tell them to him the next morning. The king thought that their dreams might reveal to him what kind of rulers his sons might make some day.

The next morning the eldest son told of a dream where his hands were outstretched and filling the palms of his hands were farms, villages, cities, and all manner of animals and people. The king thought that this was a good dream for a prince because it showed that his possessions would be bountiful and he would take care of and nurture the land. He gave the prince a fine estate.

The second prince, oddly enough, had the same dream as his older brother. The king was so pleased that he gave this son an estate as well.

The youngest son, Damian, asked to be excused from telling his dream. The king, who was known for his bad temper, insisted in anger that Damian recount his dream.

"I dreamt that you brought me a pitcher and basin to wash my hands and mother brought me a towel to dry them."

The king immediately flew into a violent rage. "Who do you think you are? Are you better than your king and queen that we should become your servants?"

Damian tried to calm his father down. "Of course not, but it was my dream, and you wanted to hear it."

The king called for his executioner and ordered him to take Damian deep into the woods, kill him, and bring back his bloody shirt.

As the two of them walked into the forest, the executioner stopped Damian and said, "I cannot kill you for I have known you since the day you were born. Give to me your shirt and your left hand." Damian did as he was requested. The executioner cut off the little finger of the boy's left hand and smeared the blood all over his shirt.

"Run as fast as you can, young prince, and don't look back." The executioner turned back toward the palace, and Damian disappeared into the forest wilderness.

Damian wandered the great forest for many months. He worked as best he could for farmers who would give him a meal and a place to sleep, but he always kept moving, looking over his shoulder in fear, wondering if the king had discovered the executioner's deceit.

One day, tired and hungry, Damian wandered deep into the forested mountains and found a great castle. As he walked toward the open gate, he saw a dragon herding a thousand goats into the courtyard. He watched as the dragon crouched down on his huge scaly legs and began to milk each and every goat, filling up an enormous bucket. He saw that the dragon had no eyes. When the beast had finished he took the bucket and drank every last drop of milk. The dragon then drove the goats into the barn, closed the door, and went into the castle.

Damian silently followed the dragon into the castle and watched as he filled a pipe with several pounds of tobacco and began to smoke. As the dragon relaxed, an idea crept into Damian's head. It seemed he needed a safe place to stay, and the dragon needed someone with eyes who could help him.

"Excuse me," he said quietly. "I was wondering if by any chance you might need a servant."

"What? Who are you?" asked the startled dragon.

"I'm just a young man with no home and no family, and much in need of food and shelter."

"Are you a hard worker?" asked the dragon. "I do need help around here, and if you're willing to work, I will treat you as if you were my own son."

The blind dragon let his claws lightly touch Damian's face and decided that it felt like an honest one.

"I will be your eyes," said Damian, "and help you in any way I can."

The two talked all afternoon, and the next day Damian started to work on the castle. There was a lot to do. Thirty-two years of spider webs filled the library, thirty-two years of bats filled the attic, thirty-two years of dirty dishes filled the kitchen, while thirty-two years of dust had to be swept from every room, for it had been thirty-two years since the dragon lost his sight.

At the end of the first week the dragon called Damian to him and said, "I have a gift for you. I know, my son, that you cannot live just on the milk of our goats as I do. This diamond wand will provide you with food whenever you want it. Wave it to the right and a table laden with food will appear; wave it to the left and it will disappear."

Damian took the wand, and true to the dragon's word, it provided the prince with the finest of foods whenever he wanted.

One day, when Damian was cleaning, he found an old flute on a shelf. He started to play a song on it and immediately everything in the room began to dance—the chairs and tables, the mouse and cat, pots and pans in the kitchen, and logs in the fireplaces, all twirling around. He looked out the window and saw that the trees and hills and fields were all dancing. When he stopped playing, everything went still.

When the dragon returned home with his goats, he told Damian of how he and the goats all had an uncontrollable urge to dance. "I danced so much that I'm completely worn out," said the old dragon.

"Father," said Damian, "let me take the goats out tomorrow. You need a good rest, and it would be a pleasant change for me."

"Thank you," said the dragon. "I could use a little rest. But you must not go near the hill to the north of the castle. You see it outside the window, with the little house on top of it surrounded by willow trees? That is the home of the witch maidens, two sisters who steal the eyes of anyone that comes close to their house. Thirty-two years ago they stole my eyes. You must promise me to be careful."

"It is only a madman who rushes into a fire and burns himself," said Damian.

"Then do not be mad, my son," said the dragon.

The next day Damian led his goats straight to the hill where the witches lived. He let his herd graze while, with the flute in his back pocket, he climbed a tree and waited. Soon the witches came running out of their house and toward the tree where Damian sat. As they got closer, Damian started to play his flute. Everything started to dance—the house and the goats, and the trees, and the fields, and the witches. As they all danced, one of the two witches tried to leap up and catch Damian, but he caught her hair and tied it to a branch. Soon, both witches were hanging by their hair, dancing in the air.

"Set us free," they begged, "and we will do anything."

"Restore my father's eyes," said Damian.

"Let us go free and we will fetch them."

"Never. Tell me where they are and I will fetch them myself."

The witches told him that the eyes were in a box and were now in the shape of two golden apples. When Damian returned, they tried to convince him to let them down.

"My father still needs his eyes. When he has them back, he will come here and release you himself."

Damian returned to the castle and gave the dragon one apple to eat. When he finished, he leapt for joy. "I can see from my right eye."

Then Damian gave his dragon father the other apple. Roaring with delight, he saw the world again as he had seen it so many years ago. He danced and sang and laughed with joy. He looked down at Damian and said, "You are the best of sons."

The dragon then flew to the tree were the witches were hanging and, with one blast of his fiery breath, turned them both into a pile of ashes.

When the dragon returned to the castle, he gave Damian a key ring with thirty-nine keys. "These are the keys to all my treasure chambers. They are yours. Take whatever it is you want, for you are my heir and everything that I have is yours."

Damian went into all thirty-nine rooms and found treasures beyond belief—gold and silver and precious jewels. There were mountains of treasure.

Damian wasn't interested in treasure, but he found a shirt made of the lightest silver cloth and trousers and shoes to match. He took a few gems and some gold coins. He found a beautiful sword of the finest steel, fitted with a hilt of gold and a scabbard encrusted with diamonds. He found chain mail so strong that nothing could pierce it, but so light he hardly felt it on his back. He gathered these things up to show his father, but as he walked toward the stairs, he saw another door. It was covered in rust and none of the keys would fit the lock.

"Father, I found a fortieth door but none of the keys would open it. What's behind the door?"

"Odds and ends, broken chairs, bottles and rubbish. Nothing you'd want to see. Besides, the key is lost."

"One man's rubbish is another man's treasure. I'd like to see that room."

"The key is lost," said the dragon.

Damian didn't believe him. "Father, there is something you are hiding from me."

The dragon sighed, and the whole castle and all the goats sighed with him. "I'm afraid that if you go into that room I will lose you forever." The dragon started to cry and Damian didn't ask again. No more was said about the room.

Then, the next morning the old dragon came to Damian and, still weeping, took a rusty key out of his ear and gave it to the prince. "Take it and unlock the door if you must, but remember that I will always love you and that my heart goes wherever you go." The dragon embraced Damian and, still sobbing, walked away.

Damian put on his new clothes and took his armor and sword with him down to the room. He opened the door. There, inside a stable, stood a beautiful mare with a coat of silver and mane and tail of gold.

"So, you have finally come, my prince. Quickly, get on my back, for we must fly like the wind."

"What is so urgent?" asked Damian.

"Your foolish father, the king, has challenged any prince or lord who wants to marry your sister to jump the great marsh that lies to the east of the castle. All have failed and many have died. Now their families have united and are marching a great army against your father. They intend to destroy him and all your kin."

When Damian heard these words, he forgot about his father's cruelty, and the dragon's tears, and thought only of saving his family. He mounted the horse and soon they were flying like the wind across the land.

They arrived at the scene of two armies locked in battle. His father's army slowly was being pushed back. Damian and the silver mare charged into battle. The dragon's sword could not be stopped and soon the opposing warriors were fleeing for their lives.

When the enemy was in full retreat, the king came over to Damian and, not recognizing his son, begged him to come back to his castle for a victory feast.

Once they arrived at the castle, Damian was given a place of honor at the high table, seated at the king's right hand. Everyone in the hall was impressed by Damian's rich mail and clothing, and the wonderful sword that hung at his side. None recognized the boy that had fled the castle so many years ago. Before they ate, the king himself brought water and a basin for Damian to wash his hands and the queen brought him a towel to dry them. Damian smiled as he remembered the dream he had all those years ago.

After the feast was underway, Damian stood before the king and asked permission to tell everyone a story. The king called for quiet and everyone waited for Damian to begin.

"Once there was a king who had three sons. One morning the king asked each son to tell what he had dreamed the night before. The youngest prince told a dream that upset the king so much that he ordered his son to be taken into the woods and killed. But the executioner who had watched the prince grow up was a kind man and could not kill the boy. So he cut off the boy's finger, dabbed the blood onto the prince's shirt, and told him to run. I am that prince." Damian took off his glove and showed the hand with the missing finger.

The king fell to his knees and begged his son's forgiveness. "You can have my throne, my crown, and all my lands," said the king.

Damian laughed. "I do not want your kingdom or your crown. I do want you to reward the executioner for sparing my life. I do want you to stop the silly game that has caused this war. I do want you to control your temper."

The king promised all of that and more, and the feast turned into a celebration not only of victory but also of the return of Damian to his family.

A few weeks later Damian was in the stables grooming the silver mare when she spoke. "Have you forgotten the one who loves you the most?"

Damian had indeed forgotten about the dragon, but in that moment all the wonderful memories of his foster father came flooding into his mind. "Let us visit him now," cried Damian.

Damian mounted the silver mare, and soon they were trotting up to the dragon's castle. There sat the old dragon, milking his goats and weeping for his lost adopted son.

Damian crept up behind the dragon and whispered, "Father, I am here."

The dragon stood up so quickly the milk went flying through the air and the goats ran in every direction.

The two of them hugged and laughed, and Damian told the dragon of all his adventures.

"I have come to return your wonderful horse," said Damian.

"All that I have is yours," declared the dragon. "Keep the horse, but please promise to visit me once in a while."

"I will visit every full moon. We will talk and laugh and tell stories."

And so, throughout the years, Damian kept his promise, and the dragon never again shed tears of unhappiness, only tears of joy.

Notes

This is an unusual story for a European dragon tale because the dragon is kind and helpful. In Asia the dragons are usually beneficial, but in Europe they tend to be evil and aggressive. Dragon tales are found worldwide. Dragons in China are depicted usually as not having wings but they can still fly. When they reach the age of 1,000 years, they can grow wings if they desire.

—DK

Zal, the White Haired

A folktale from Ancient Persia

Sam was a great warrior and the king of Zabulestan, respected as a just ruler of his kingdom. His young wife was expecting their first child and the palace was filled with excitement as her day of delivery approached. But when the day arrived, there was no joy in the queen's chambers. Her child had been born beautiful, with strong long limbs and a smile that told of an easy disposition, but his hair was pure white.

No one knew if this was a good or bad omen, whether the gods were pleased or not with the king, whether the child was cursed or blessed.

Now the old midwife consoled the young queen, who was afraid to tell her husband of their strange child. Soon the two women could hide the truth no longer. The midwife offered to go to the king and give him the news.

She found the king in his throne room handing out justice and settling disputes. As he finished she approached him and said, "Rejoice my king for you have been blessed with a son. He is as beautiful as any father could hope for and his strong lungs and limbs tell us that he will be a great and powerful warrior."

The king leapt to his feet and yelled with joy. The nurse went on, "He is without blemish from the top of his head to the toes of his feet. He only differs from other babes in one way, and should not the son of a king differ from his subjects? His hair is silvery white, as pale as the moonlight or the snow that crowns the mountains. Give thanks to Ormuzd for the beauty and health of your son."

The king stopped smiling. "What are you saying woman? No babe has ever been born with white hair. Is this a joke?"

"No, my lord, it is no joke," she whispered.

"Take me to him."

Sam looked down at the sleeping babe resting in his mother's arms and saw that indeed his hair was as white as snow. "This child cannot be a gift from Ormuzd but a joke sent to me by Ahriman to taunt me and ridicule me before the world."

Then Sam lifted the child and prayed to his god. "Forgive me, Ormuzd, for any mistakes I've made or if I acted cruelly or unjustly. I will rid myself and my people of this abomination." He had the babe taken out to the desert and left at the foot of the Elburz Mountains to die alone and abandoned.

The child lay on the hard, stony ground in the burning sun. His cries became softer and softer. But, just as he was about to take his last breath, his cries came to the ears of the great magical bird Simurgh as she flew in the sky looking for food for her own babes.

She swooped down, her huge black wings casting a shadow over the new born, and gently snatched him up in her talons and flew to her nest on the very top of Mount Damavand, the highest point in the mountains. She placed the tiny babe in among her own hatchlings, but even though they were hungry, they would not harm the babe. The Simurgh flew off again and came back with a fawn for them to eat. When she looked into her nest, she saw that her offspring and the human child were huddled together. They had accepted the child as one of them.

Now, the great Simurgh also accepted the boy. She fed him tender strips of meat and cleaned him with her beak. Her fledglings flourished and so did he, growing strong and straight, fast and keen of eye. As his adopted brothers and sisters flew through the air, the boy ran like the wind across mountaintops and hills and through valleys and woods. As time passed, travelers often caught sight of a young man racing across the sands or the hills, and slowly word spread of the wild boy who lived with the magical bird Simurgh.

Finally, after many years, word of the strange youngster reached the ears of Sam, the king. The merchant who spoke of him described a strong young man with hair the color of silver or moonbeams. Sam knew this must be his son. The king had hated himself for giving in to superstition. Just days after abandoning his son, he had searched for him but had not found a trace. Now he had hope and was determined to seek out the white-haired youth.

Sam came to the foothills of the Elburz Mountains. With the eyes of a great hunter he could see the nest of the mighty Simurgh, almost touching the clouds. He could see the giant bird and a youth sitting next to her with hair as white as snow. Sam tried to climb the mountain but every way was blocked and each attempt ended in failure.

Finally, Sam knelt and prayed once again to Ormuzd. "Great god, you have spared my son and given him life when I ordered death. If he is truly mine, then let me stand beside him that I might speak to him and hold him close."

At the top of the mountain Simurgh saw him as he prayed and, with her magical wisdom, she knew who he was and why he was there. She turned to the boy and said, "At the foot of the mountain there is a great king. He is Sam and he is your father, the one who left you to die. He repents that deed and he is here seeking forgiveness. He has a father's love, a great kingdom, and respect and devotion among men. I would have you stay here with me forever for I love you as much as I have loved any of my brood. But you are a man and you should live among men. The time has come for us to part." And saying that, the great bird took the boy in her talons and spread her wings and flew down the mountain and set him down before Sam.

Simurgh could see the father in the boy. The silvery white hair that Sam had thought to be a curse was now so beautiful that the king could scarcely speak.

Before flying away, Simurgh spoke again to the boy, "You are no less my child than the first day I found you. My love and guidance will always be yours." Then the great bird lifted her black wings and with her iron beak she plucked a feather from her wing. "Take this feather, and if ever you need my help, burn the feather and I will know you need me and will fly to your aid." With those words she spread her wings and flew off into the sky above the mountains.

Sam took his son home to the palace where his mother and younger brothers and sisters welcomed him and held a great feast in his honor. Sam named the young man Zal. From Sam, Zal learned to be a great warrior and protector of his people, a just ruler, and a friend to all. From his mother, Zal learned kindness, forgiveness, mercy, and the strength to listen to all. Indeed, Zal became a great man loved by his people and honored for his wisdom by all he met.

Notes

There are many great birds in the mythology and folktales of people across the earth. The great bird The Rukh is featured in the tales of "Sinbad the Sailor" in The Arabian Nights. *In Native American mythology, in*

Midwestern America, there is the Piasa Bird documented by the French explorer Pére Marquette, who saw a painting of it on the side of a cliff overlooking the Illinois River. The Thunderbird is also featured in Native American mythology while the phoenix is found in Eastern European tales.

—DK

The Grateful Fox Fairy

A folktale from China

Far away and just as long ago, there lived a boy named Yang Le. He grew up with his devoted mother and his father, a general in the army. When he was eighteen, tragedy struck and he lost both parents in a terrible accident. His father's cousin, Wen Sing, kindly invited him to live in the courts of his palace.

Wen Sing welcomed Yang Le and found a place for him. One balmy day in the courtyard, Yang Le happened upon Mai Mai, the fair daughter of Wen Sing, as she walked in the garden with her aunt and two young women. Mai Mai was as beautiful as the plum blossom for which she was named. Her aunt, who served as her guardian, taught her the rules for good maidenly behavior and she never let Mai Mai out of her sight. The graceful Mai Mai walked with a serene smile, but when she saw Yang Le, her eyes widened and she blushed before casting her eyes downward with a little smile.

Yang Le was so taken with Mai Mai's charm that he could think of nothing else. Mai Mai never left the inner courts except to walk the lush gardens with her ever-present aunt or female cousins. The only occasions Yang Le saw his beloved Mai Mai was at family feast days or by chance in the gardens. At these times, Mai Mai would sneak a peek at Yang Le and beam a glorious smile that lit up her warm brown eyes. Yang Le longed to speak with her, for it seemed that she fancied him too.

In his lonely room, Yang Le wrote long love poems about Mai Mai to sooth his aching heart. Late one night in unbearable heat, Yang Le walked along the garden path in hopes of catching a cool breeze. In the moonlight, he caught sight of an exquisite silhouette moving toward him. It was the lovely lady, Mai Mai.

She blushed and said, "I should have asked my aunt before leaving our bed, but it is so humid; I hoped for some relief in the garden."

They spoke for a long while and Yang Le found that his sweet cousin cared for him as much as he loved her. But Mai Mai's father had promised her hand in marriage to the son of a wealthy neighbor and would never consent to Yang Le's proposal of marriage. Still, they agreed to meet secretly at night under the plum trees. Overtime, they grew deeper in love.

Then, late one night, a watchman walking outside the gardens overheard their whispers. Peering through the gates, he saw Yang Le with Mai Mai. The next morning, he ran to tell Wen Sing.

"How can this be?" Wen Sing raged at Mai Mai's aunt. "You are supposed to attend my daughter at all times. What have you to say for yourself?"

Shocked, Mai Mai's guardian replied, "Honorable brother, this maiden could not be Mai Mai! I sleep in the same bed with her and she sleeps on the inside by the wall. I often wake up and check to see if she is sleeping beside me."

But Wen Sing would not be calmed. When he questioned his daughter, Mai Mai simply lowered her head. She would not speak for fear that her beloved Yang Le would be beaten. Wen Sing threw up his hands and went to his wife.

"Something is going on but we cannot prove it," she said. "We must send Yang Le away."

Wen Sing escorted Yang Le to the outside gate, handed him a bag of money, and sent him on his way. After wandering for many days in search of a new home, Yang Le found a pagoda with seven small curving roofs that stood near the edge of the town. Finding it empty, he moved in.

Time passed slowly for Yang Le until one day, four strong men carrying a sedan chair stopped at his door. As the richly brocaded curtains opened, out stepped Mai Mai dressed in a red bridal gown. The men unpacked her possessions as Yang Le stood in disbelief.

"My father has consented to our marriage," Mai Mai said with a radiant smile. "I was brought here by my uncle Chu, who is the general in this part of the country."

Yang Le could not believe his eyes and was greatly puzzled by Wen Sing's change of heart. The next day, he set out to visit General Chu and thank him for escorting Mai Mai to her new home. Overjoyed at his great fortune Yang Le wished to show his gratitude.

But Mai Mai's uncle was confused by Yang Le's visit. "Mai Mai is still with her father," he said. "I did not bring her here. My brother would have told me if his daughter came to my region."

"Come," said Yang Le, "and see for yourself."

Of course when General Chu saw Mai Mai, his mouth dropped open in amazement. Indeed, the fair bride before him was his brother's daughter. In haste, the general traveled with the young couple to the big city where Wen Sing lived. There, he sought out his brother to tell him of his daughter and her new husband.

"But my daughter has never been outside the gate. How could this be?" exclaimed Wen Sing.

Again, he called his wife and Mai Mai's guardian. They shook their heads in disbelief.

"Oh," cried the mother suddenly, "this must be the doing of a fox fairy who has taken on the likeness of our daughter to create mischief. People will think Mai Mai is an improper maiden. We must act quickly to avoid a scandal. Mai Mai must marry Yang Le. There is nothing else we can do."

Wen Sing and General Chu nodded in agreement. This was the only way to solve the problem and save face. So General Chu brought Yang Le and Mai Mai into the family hall. As they entered, Yang Le held his hand to his heart for he was in utter shock. There, standing beside her parents, was another Mai Mai. So identical were the ladies that even Wen Sing and his wife could not see a difference.

Yang Le's bride smiled and pointed to Mai Mai, "There stands the true daughter of Wen Sing. I am a fox fairy who is returning a good deed."

Then turning to Yang Le she said, "Long ago, Yang Han, your grandfather, was hunting deer near my mountain cave when an arrow pierced my leg. His servants brought me to him and he staunched the blood and bandaged my leg. Then, the good general set me free. I am repaying my debt to your grandfather through you, Yang Le, for I have not forgotten his kindness."

The Wen family stood in mute shock. The fox fairy turned to the family and continued, "I saw that Yang Le loved your daughter and I knew that the old man in the moon long ago had joined their ankles together with the red cord of marriage. It was meant to be. So I helped. As I am over a thousand years old, I can assume the shape of any human I choose. It was I who spoke for Mai Mai in the garden with Yang Le and posed as Yang Le's bride. Now, they will marry and my work is done. I shall not return."

The maiden fairy faded into the air and in her place stood a red fox who quickly turned a somersault, striking the floor with its tail that sent sparks flying everywhere. Then the fox disappeared from the room.

In the Hall of the Ancestors, Yang Le and Mai Mai were wed that very day and they celebrated their marriage in proper fashion by eating rice cakes and toasting with wedding wine.

Notes

The fox is an animal native to China. They are noted to be quick, intelligent, curious, and adaptable creatures. In Chinese folklore and mythology, the fox is similar to the European fairy. It has the power to change its shape, usually into human form and often as a woman. The Huli jing, *or fox spirit, reflects the Chinese culture's attitudes toward obligation. If someone does you a kindness, then you are expected to reciprocate in the same manner.*

In this tale, the fox fairy repays her debt through her assistance to the grandchild of the man who mended her leg and set her free. If a fox fairy has been badly treated or sees misbehavior, then they will behave vindictively toward the perpetrator of the deed.

—KB

The Gift of the Unicorn

A folktale from China

In the olden times it was said that Ki-lin, the unicorn, would appear before the emperors who possessed wisdom and compassion. When the Middle Kingdom fell, chaos ruled as one state attacked another. Peace was shattered as kings fought for land and wealth and the Ki-lin vanished from this violent and selfish world. The unicorn was not seen for centuries until the sixth century BCE.

In the town of Chufu at the foot of the sacred mountain Tai Shan, there lived a woman. She was a wise, good woman and kind to all her neighbors. But for all the joy she brought others, she held a deep sorrow. She could not bear a son for her husband. Without a son there would be no one to worship at the ancestral grave tablets and there would be no life after death for the ancestors if there was no one to remember them.

She prayed and begged the gods to have pity on her and give her a son. No matter how hard she prayed no son was born. Finally, she decided to climb Tai Shan and pray at the temple at the summit one more time.

She knew, as a few others did, that unicorns lived on the mountain. As she walked up the steep path, she unknowingly stepped into the footprints of the Ki-lin. This called the unicorn to her and it stood facing her on the path. The Ki-lin had the body of a deer, the hooves of a horse, the tail of an ox, and its mottled fur was red, blue, yellow, white, and black. The good woman looked into those deep eyes and felt she might drown in their darkness. The Ki-lin crooked its head one way and then the other. Softly, it called her name and its voice sounded like the music of chimes. Slowly, the wise Ki-lin knelt in front of her. It placed a piece of jade gently at her feet. The woman picked it up and looked at the words carved on the stone. "Your son shall be a ruler without a throne."

When the woman looked up, the Ki-lin was gone, but the jade was still in her hand. She knew magic had touched her that day.

Months later, she and her husband had a son, whom they named Kung Fu Tzu, Confucius. Even as a child, he was wise and gentle. Confucius became a great teacher. He and his followers walked the length of China teaching any who would listen. The people lived by his wisdom. He was as influential as any emperor. Indeed, he was a ruler without a throne.

Notes

Confucius is regarded as one of the wisest men that ever lived in China. His followers spread his message of wisdom to all corners of the land. He was an advisor to the emperor and many other leaders and scholars.

The footprints of a unicorn are invisible, but if you do step in them, the creature will appear to you. Unlike the European unicorn, which needs to defend itself, the Chinese Ki-lin cannot be harmed by men, so its single horn is soft and unfit for battle. The Ki-lin is the emperor of the animals of earth. It does not eat any living thing including grass and leaves and it will not step on a living creature, not even one as small as an ant.

—DK

Section 6

Not One or the Other

Why Platypus Is Special

A folktale from Aborigines of Australia

In the Dreamtime, the Creator made three different types of animals. First, he created the mammals that were told that they were to live on land. He gave them thick hides and fur to keep them warm. Then, he made the birds, and they were to live in the sky. He gave them wings that took them to the heavens, and he gave the mothers the ability to lay eggs. Then, he made the fish that would dwell in water. He gave them gills that allowed them to breathe.

When the Creator was finished, he found that many of the wonderful parts he had given mammals, birds, and fish were left over, so he put them together and created platypus. Now, these unique creatures are like no other animal on earth. They have fur like a mammal, they swim under water like a fish, and they lay eggs like a bird.

For a long time all the animals of creation lived happily together. Eventually, though, they began to quarrel. Each group thought it was the best and most important and was out to prove it.

The mammals had a meeting to declare war on the birds and fish. The kangaroo stood up and cried, "We mammals are the greatest. We are special because we have fur."

The kangaroo's wife said, "Yes. But the platypus has fur, too."

The mammals thought about this and decided to ask the platypus to join their war against the fish and birds. The platypus listened very carefully and said, "Thank you for visiting me and asking me to be one of your family. I'll think about it."

A few days later the fish had a meeting. The Murray cod jumped out of the water and landed with an impressive whack. "We fish are special because we swim under water. We are the best."

But the cod's wife said, "What about the platypus? He spends most of his time under water."

The fish decided to go and visit the platypus and ask him to join their war against the mammals and birds. The platypus listened very carefully and said, "Thank you for the invitation to be one of your family. I'll think about it."

Soon the birds held a meeting and the eagle spread his massive wings and beat the air, and it sounded like a storm. "We are special," cried the eagle, "for only we can fly and lay eggs."

"What about the platypus?" said the eagle's wife. "She lays eggs, too."

The birds went to the platypus and asked him if he would join their war against the mammals and the fish. The platypus listened very carefully and said, "Thank you for the invitation to be one of your family. I'll think about it."

Now, the platypus thought it over for several days. Finally, the birds and fish and mammals got tired of waiting. They all crowded around his home and began shouting, "Join our family. No, join our family."

"We are special," cried the birds.

"We are the best," cried the fish.

"We are wonderful," cried the mammals.

Together they all shouted, "Which group will you join?"

Finally, the platypus slowly came out of his home on the bank of the billabong. All the animals fell silent.

"I've given your words and offers a great deal of thought," said the platypus. "I am a part of each of you and part of all of you. That's how I want it to stay, so I will not be joining any group."

There was a great deal of grumbling among all the animals.

"When the Creator made us, he made each of us unique," said the platypus, "so we are all special. We are different from each other, but not better. We should respect and celebrate that which makes us unique, that which makes us different. We should live together in peace."

The fish and the birds and the mammals all thought that this was a wonderful idea. The platypus was wise and had shown them a way to live together happily.

Standing at the edge of the crowd of animals was a man, a hunter. He had listened to everything that had been said and was impressed by the wisdom that the platypus had shown. He carried the ideas that the platypus had spoken to the animals back to his village and shared them with his people.

From that day on no Aboriginal Australian would ever hunt and kill a platypus. Their wisdom is too important to lose.

――――――――

Notes

The platypus is found in eastern Australia and Tasmania. As the story illustrates, it is one of the most unique animals in the world. Australia is a continent as well as a nation and has a diverse environment.

—DK

Appendix

Table of Animals and Countries

Story	Animal	Country
Arion and the Dolphin	Dolphin	Ancient Greece
Zal, the White Haired	Simurgh	Ancient Persia
The Three Girls and the Johnnycakes	Birds, woodland creatures	Appalachia, USA
The Maiden and the Puma	Puma	Argentina
Why Platypus Is Special	Platypus	Australia
The Helpful Animals	Dog, cat, mongoose	Burma
The Waiting Maid and the Parrot	Parrot	China
The Grateful Fox Fairy	Fox	China
The Gift of the Unicorn	Unicorn	China
Frog Princess	Frog	Croatia
General Dog and His Army	Dog, fox, bear, wolf, mole, kumrekusha, mouse, hare	Croatia
Mighty Mikko	Fox	Finland
The Fisherman and His Wife	Fish (flounder)	Germany
The Queen Bee	Ants, bees, ducks	Germany
The Golden Crab	Crab	Greece
Damian and the Dragon	Dragon, horse	Greece
The Rooster and the Sultan	Rooster	Hungary
The Brahmini and the Mongoose	Mongoose, snake	India
The Raja's Son and Princess Labam	Ants, tiger	India

(*continued*)

Story	Animal	Country
The Little Red Fish and the Clog of Gold	Fish	Iraq
The Grateful Wolf	Wolf	Japan
The Thankful Badger Family	Badgers	Japan
Crane Child	Crane	Japan
Yogodayu and the Army of Bees	Bees	Japan
The Samurai and the Sea Turtle	Sea turtle	Japan
The Boy Who Drew Cats	Cats	Japan
The Birds' Garden	Birds	Kazakhstan
The Pheasants and the Bell	Pheasants, snake	Korea
How the Wasp Lost His Voice	Wasp, swallow	Mongolia
Maui and the Birds	Birds	New Zealand
How Man Found a Friend	Snake, elephant, monkey, dog	Nigeria
The Man, the Dove, and the Hawk	Dove, hawk	Nigeria
The Two Stepsisters	Sheep, cow, birds	Norway
The White Spider's Gift	Spider	Paraguay
The Youth Who Made Friends with the Beasts and the Birds	Birds, snake, fox, cougars, tapir, deer	Peru
The King's Youngest Son	Fish, deer, eagle, fox	Republic of Georgia
Blind Man's Bluff	Mouse	Russia
Emelya, the Fool	Fish (pike)	Russia
The Leshi Cat	Mythical creature	Russia
Oleshek, the Deer with the Golden Antlers	Deer	Sami
The Seal Hunter and the Merman	Merman	Scotland
Marko Kraljevic and the Eagle	Eagle	Serbia
Snake's Blessing	Snake	Swahili
The Man and the Muskrat	Muskrat	Tanzania
The Young Man Who Refused to Kill	Horse	Tibet
The Grateful Alligators	Alligator	USA
The Dragons of Ha Long Bay	Dragons	Vietnam

Story Sources

Section 1: Creatures of the Land

The Grateful Wolf (Japan)

Motif: B520

"The Wolf's Debt" on page 35 in Kevin Strauss, *The Song of the Wolf: Legends and Folktales from around the World* (self-published, 2005). ISBN 1571662731.

"The Wolf's Reward" on page 20 in Keigo Seki, ed., *Folktales of Japan* (Chicago, IL: University of Chicago Press, 1963). ISBN 0226746151.

"The Mountain Wolf's Debt" appears on Kevin Strauss, *The Mountain Wolf's Gift: Wolf Tales from around the World* (CD) (Rochester, MN: Naturestory Recordings, 2003). 1001CD.

The Maiden and the Puma (Argentina)

Motif: B576

"The Girl and the Puma" on page 27 in Jane Yolen, *Not One Damsel in Distress: World Folktales for Strong Girls* (San Diego, CA: Silver Whistle, Harcourt, Inc., 2000). ISBN 9780152020477. 116 pp.

"The Girl and the Puma" on page 23 in M. A. Jagendorf and R. S. Boggs, *The King of the Mountain: A Treasury of Latin American Folktales* (New York: Vanguard Press, Inc., 1960). ISBN 081490338X. 313 pp.

Oleshek, the Deer with the Golden Antlers (Sami)

Motif: B430

"Oleshek, the Deer with the Golden Antlers" on page 15 in Bonnie C. Marshall, *Far North Tales: Stories from the People of the Arctic Circle* (Santa Barbara, CA: Libraries Unlimited, 2011). ISBN 9781591587613. 290 pp.

The Man and the Muskrat (Tanzania)

Motif: B360

"The Man and the Muskrat" on page 69 in Roger D. Abrahams, *African Folktales* (New York: Pantheon Books, 1983). ISBN 0394502361.

"The Man and the Muskrat" on page 56 of Roy Willis, *There Was a Certain Man: Spoken Art of the Fipa* (Oxford, England: Oxford University Press).

The Thankful Badger Family (Japan)

Motif: B430

"The Helpful Badger" on page 9 in Laurence Yep, *Tree of Dreams: Ten Tales from the Garden of Night* (Mahwah, NJ: BridgeWater Books of Troll Associates, 1995). ISBN 0816734984. 94 pp.

"The Goblin Fox and Badger and Other Witch Animals of Japan" on page 53 in U. A. Casal, *Asian Folklore Studies,* vol. XVIII (1959).

"The Badger in Japanese Folklore" on page 3 in Violet H. Harada, *Asian Folklore Studies,* vol. 35, No. 1 (1976).

The Brahmini and the Mongoose (India)

Motif: B331.2.1

"The Brahmin's Wife and the Mongoose" on page 106 in Idries Shah, *World Tales: The Extraordinary Coincidence of Stories Told in All Times, in All Places* (New York: Harcourt Brace Jovanovich, Inc., 1979). ISBN 015199434X. 258 pp.

"The Brahmin's Wife and the Mongoose" on page 162 in Mrs. Howard [Georgiana] Kingscote and Pandit Natêsá Sástrî, *Tales of the Sun; or Folklore of Southern India* (London and Calcutta: W. H. Allen and Company, 1890).

How Man Found a Friend (Nigeria)

Motif: B300

"How Man Found a Friend" on page 61 in Gavin McIntosh, *Hausaland Tales from the Nigerian Marketplace* (North Haven, CT: Linnet Books, 2002). ISBN 0208025235. 128 pp.

"The White Man and Snake" a variant on page 101 in James A. Honey, *South African Folk-Tales* (New York: The Baker and Taylor Company, 1910). 151 pp.

"The White Man and Snake" a variant on page 28 in Robert Nye's *Classic Folktales from around the World* (London: Random House, 1996). ISBN 1858913306. 605 pp.

Mighty Mikko (Finland)

Motif: B435.1

"Mighty Mikko" on page 33 in Atelia Clarkson and Gilbert B. Cross, *World Folktales* (New York: Charles Scribner's Sons, 1980). ISBN 0684177633.

"Mighty Mikko" on page 27 in Parker Filmore, *Mighty Mikko: A Book of Finnish Fairy Tales and Folk Tales* (New York: Harcourt, Brace and Company, 1922). 314 pages.

Tormod Kinnes. "Mighty Mikko (The Grateful Fox)." *Finnish Folktales.* http://oaks.nvg.org/fintal1.html#woodsman-fox (accessed August 17, 2015).

The Young Man Who Refused to Kill (Tibet)

Motif: B651.1B

"The Young Man Who Refused to Kill" on page 118 in John Elder, ed., and Hertha D. Wong, *Family of Erath & Sky: Indigenous Tales of Nature from around the World* (Boston: Beacon Press Books, 1994). ISBN 0807085286. 323 pp.

"The Young Man Who Refused to Kill" on page 76 in Frederick and Audrey Hyde-Chambers, *Tibetan Folk Tales* (Boston: Shambhala Publications, Inc., 1981). ISBN 1570620903. 208 pp.

Snake's Blessing (Swahili)

Motif: B491.1

"Snake Magic" on page 84 in Kathleen Arnott, *African Myths and Legends* (New York: Oxford University Press, 1962). ISBN 0192741152. 211 pp.

"Blessing or Property" on page 391 in Edward Steere, *Swahili Tales as Told by Natives of Zanzibar* (London: Bell and Daldy, 1870). 504 pp.

Blind Man's Bluff (Russia)

Motif: Q2.1.3B, H1539.1

"Blindman's Bluff" on page 121 in Ruth Stotter, *The Golden Axe and Other Folktales of Compassion and Greed* (Oakland, CA: Regent Press, Typeset/Layout Stotter Press, 1998). ISBN 0943565162. 183 pp.

A variant of the story is "Daughter and Stepdaughter" on page 109 in Janet Higonnet-Schnopper, *Tales from Atop a Russian Stove* (Chicago: Albert Whitman and Co., 1973). ISBN 0807577553. 160 pp.

"Daughter and Stepdaughter" on page 278 in Aleksandr Afanas'ev, *Russian Fairy Tales* (New York: Pantheon, 1973). ISBN 0394730909. 661 pp.

The White Spider's Gift (Paraguay)

Motif: B489.1

"The White Spider's Gift" on page 43 in Genevieve Barlow, *Latin American Tales: From the Pampas to the Pyramids of Mexico* (Chicago: Rand McNally and Company, 1966). LCCN 66008455. 144 pages.

"The White Spider's Gift" from Francisco Barnoya Galvez, *La Leyenda del Nanduti* (Santiago de Chile: Empresa Editora Zig-Zag, S.A., 1939).

Amy Friedman and Meredith Johnson. "A Spider's Gift (A South American Folktale)." *Uexpress.* 1996. http://www.uexpress.com/tell-me-a-story/1996/9/1/the-spiders-gift-a-south-american (accessed August 18, 2015).

Section 2: Creatures of the Sky

How the Wasp Lost His Voice (Mongolia)

Motif: B451.7

"How the Wasp Lost His Voice" on page 85 in Hillary Rose Metternich, *Mongolian Folktales* (Boulder, CO: Avery Press, 1996). ISBN 09373 21060. 131 pp.

"Who Has the Sweetest Flesh on Earth" on page 223 in Inea Bushnaq, *Arab Folktales* (New York: Pantheon Books, 1986). ISBN 0394501047. 386 pp.

"The Swallow and the Wasp" on page 10 in D. Altangerel, *Mongolian Folktales and Legends* (Ulaanbaatar, Mongolia: SOD Press, 2002).

The Birds' Garden (Kazakhstan)

Motif: B450

"The Magic Garden" on page 50 in Mary Lou Masey, *Stories of the Steppes, Kazakh Folktales* (New York: David McKay Company, 1968). LCCN 68020183. 142 pp.

"The Magic Garden of the Poor" on page 129 in Margaret Read MacDonald, *Earth Care: World Folktales to Talk About* (North Haven, CT: Linnet Books, 1999). ISBN 0208024263. 162 pp.

"The Magic Garden" on page 56 in Dawn Casey, *The Barefoot Book of Earth Tales* (Cambridge, MA: Barefoot Books, 2009). ISBN 9781846862243. 97 pp.

Maui and the Birds (Maori–New Zealand)

Motif: A728.2

"Maui Snares the Sun" on page 199 in Johannes C. Andersen, *Myths and Legends of the Polynesians* (New York: Dover Publications, 1995). ISBN 9780486285825.

"Maui and the Birds" on page 117 in Kiri Te Kanawa, *Land of the Long White Cloud* (New York: Arcade Publishing, 1989). ISBN 1559 700467.

Marko Kraljevic and the Eagle (Serbia)

Motif: B360

"Marko Kraljevic and the Falcon" on page 58 in D. H. Low, *The Ballads of Marko Kraljevic* (New York: Greenwood Press, 1968). LCCN 69010123. 196 pp.

"Prince Marko and the Hawk" on page 36 in Anne Pennington and Peter Levi, *Marko the Prince: Serbo-Croat Heroic Songs* (London: Gerald Duckworth and Company, 1984). ISBN 071561715X. 173 pp.

The Man, the Dove, and the Hawk (Nigeria)

Motif: B375.3

"The Man, the Hawk and the Dove" on page 37 of Barbara and Warren Walker, *Nigerian Folk Tales* (New Brunswick, New Jersey: Rutgers University Press, 1961). LCCN 61010268.

"King Sivi" on page 125 in Rafe Martin, *The Hungry Tigress: Buddhist Myths, Legends & Jatake Tales* (Cambridge, MA: Yellow Moon Press, 1999). ISBN 0938756524.

Crane Child (Japan)

Motif: B652.2.1

"The Crane Wife" on page 77 in Keigo Seki, *Folktales of Japan* (Chicago: The University of Chicago Press, 1963). LCCN 63013071. 221 pp.

"The Crane Maiden" on page 41 in Rafe Martin, *Mysterious Tales of Japan* (New York: G.P. Putnam's Sons, 1996). ISBN 039922677X. 74 pp.

"The Crane Wife" on page 337 in Raymond E. Jones & Jon C. Stott, *A World of Stories: Traditional Tales for Children* (Oxford, England: Oxford University Press, 2006). ISBN 019541988X. 544 pp.

The Pheasants and the Bell (Korea)

Motif: B365.0.1

"The Pheasants and the Bell" on page 96 in Zong In-Sob, *Folktales from Korea* (Elizabeth, NJ: Hollym International Corporation, 1984). ISBN 0930878264. 257 pp.

"The Grateful Magpies" on page 145 in Suzanne Crowder Han, *Korean Folk & Fairy Tales* (Elizabeth, NJ: Hollym International Corporation, 1992). ISBN 0930878043. 256 pp.

The Waiting Maid and the Parrot (China)

Motif: B469.9

"The Waiting Maid's Parrot" on page 9 in Moss Roberts, *Chinese Fairy Tales and Fantasies* (New York: Pantheon Books, 1979). ISBN 039442039X. 260 pp.

"The Waiting Maid's Parrot" on page 90 Jane Yolen, *Favorite Folktales from around the World* (New York: Pantheon Books, 1986). ISBN 0613181042. 498 pp.

The Rooster and the Sultan (Hungary)

Motif: B450

"The Cock and the Sultan of Turkey" on page 116 in Vladislav Stanovsky and Jan Vladislav, *The Twilight Hour: Legends, Fables and Fairy Tales from All Over the World* (London: Paul Hamlyn Publisher, 1961). 480 pp.

"The Clever Little Rooster" on page 39 in Peter Hargitai, *Magyar Tales* (Amherst, MA: University of Massachusetts International Studies Program, 1989). ISBN 09633161992. 66 pp.

Yogodayu and the Army of Bees (Japan)

Motif: B481.3

"How Yogodayu Won a Battle" on page 116 in Richard Gordon Smith, *Ancient Tales and Folklore of Japan* (London: Bracken Books, 1986). ISBN 0946495785. 361 pp.

"Yogodayu and the Army of Bees" on page 65 in John Matthews, *The Barefoot Book of Knights* (Cambridge, MA: Barefoot Books, 2002). ISBN 9781846863073. 80 pp.

Section 3: Creatures of the Water

The Samurai and the Sea Turtle (Japan)

Motif: A375.8

"Turtle Returns the Gift" on page 145 in Michael Caduto, *Earth Tales from around the World* (Golden, CO: Fulcrum Publishing, 1997). ISBN 1555919685. 192 pp.

"The Grateful Turtle" on page 152 in Royall Tyler, *Japanese Tales* (New York: Pantheon Books, 1987). ISBN 0394521900. 341 pp.

Frog Princess (Croatia)

Motif: B604.5

"The Frog Princess" on page 119 in Aleksandr Afanas'ev, *Russian Fairy Tales* (New York: Pantheon Books, 1945). ISBN 039449914X. 662 pp.

"The Frog Princess" on page 122 in Barbara J. Suwyn, *The Magic Egg & Other Tales from Ukraine* (Englewood, CO: Libraries Unlimited, 1997). ISBN 1563084252. 222 pp.

"The Frog" on page 246 in Andrew Lang, *The Violet Fairy Book* (Charleston, SC: Bibliobazaar). ISBN 9780554290195. 303 pp.

Arion and the Dolphin (Ancient Greece)

Motif: B551.1

"Arion and the Friendly Dolphin" on page 183 in Jason Cressey, *Deep Voices: The Wisdom of Whales & Dolphin Tales* (Victoria, Canada: Trafford Publishing, 20099). ISBN 1425141129. 591 pp.

"Arion" on page 176 of Richard Martin, editor, *Bullfinch's Mythology* (New York: Harper Collins, 1991). ISBN 0062700251. 732 pp.

"Arion" on page 74 in Michael Grant and John Hazel, *Who's Who in Classical Mythology* (London: Weidenfeld & Nicolson Ltd., 1973). ISBN 0297766007. 447 pp.

The Golden Crab (Greece)

Motif: B102.8

"The Golden Crab" on page 44 in Andrew Lang, *The Yellow Fairy Book* (Fairfield, IA: 1st World Library, 2007). ISBN 9781421844183. 392 pp.

"The Golden Crab" on page 256 in Thomas A. Green, *The Greenwood Library of World Folktales* (Westport, CT: Greenwood Press, 2008). ISBN 9780313337864. 427 pp.

The Fisherman and His Wife (Germany)

Motif: B375.1

"The Fisherman and His Wife" on page 200 in Idries Shah, *World Folktales* (New York: Harcourt Brace Jovanovich, 1979). ISBN 015199434X. 259 pp.

The Fisherman and His Wife" on page 65 in Jack Zipes, *The Complete Fairy Tales of the Brothers Grimm* (New York: Bantam Books, 2002). ISBN 0553382160. 762 pp.

Emelya, the Fool (Russia)

Motif: B375.1.3

"Emelya the Simpleton" on page 46 in Aleksandr Afanas'ev, *Russian Fairy Tales* (New York: Pantheon Books, 1973). ISBN 0394730909. 663 pp.

"Ivan the Fool and the Magic Pike" on page 18 in James Riordan, *Russian Folk-Tales* (Oxford, England: Oxford University Press, 2000). ISBN 0192745360. 96 pp.

"Omelya and the Pike" on page 35 in Arthur Ransome, *The War of the Birds and Beasts & Other Russian Tales* (London: Jonathan Cape, 1984). ISBN 0224022156. 112 pp.

The Little Red Fish and the Clog of Gold (Iraq)

Motif: A510

"The Little Red Fish and the Clog of Gold" on page 104 in Judy Sierra, *Cinderella* (Phoenix, AZ: Oryx Press, 1992). ISBN 0897747275. 178 pp.

"The Little Red Fish and the Clog of Gold" on page 181 in Inea Bushnaq, *Arab Folktales* (New York: Pantheon Books, 1986). ISBN 0394501047. 386 pp.

The Grateful Alligators (Mississippi River, USA)

Motif: B590

"The Grateful Alligators" on page 32 in B.A. Botkin, *A Treasury of Mississippi Folklore* (New York: Crown Publishers, 1955). LCCN 55010172. 620 pp.

"The Grateful Alligators" on page 190 in Melville D. Landon, *Wit and Humor of the Age* (Chicago: Star Publishing Company, 1901).

Section 4: Creatures Working Together

The Youth Who Made Friends with the Beasts and the Birds (Peru)

Motif: B216.5

"The Youth Who Made Friends with the Beasts and the Birds" on page 27 in Frances Carpenter, *South American Wonder Tales* (Chicago: Follett Publishing Company, 1969). ISBN 0695482149. 192 pp.

Additional version, "The Myth of Huathlacuri" can be found on page 207 in Lewis Spence, *Myths of Mexico and Peru* (New York: Cosimo Classics, 2010). ISBN 1616404337. 450 pp.

The King's Youngest Son (Republic of Georgia)

Motif: H321B

"The Fisherman's Son" on page 183 in Eric and Nancy Protter, ed., *Folk and Fairy Tales of Far-Off Lands* (New York: Duell, Sloan and Pearce, 1965). LCCN 65026811. 196 pp.

"The Fisherman's Son: Adapted from a Georgian Folktale" in Mirra Ginsburg, *The Fisherman's Son: Adapted from a Georgian Folktale* (New York: Greenwillow Books, 1979). ISBN 0688802168. 33 pp.

"The Prince Who Befriended the Beasts" on page 35 in Michael Berman, *Georgia through Its Folktales* (Hants, UK: John Hunt Publishing, 2010). ISBN 9781846942792. 160 pp.

"The Prince Who Befriended the Beasts" on page 135 in Marjory Wardrop, *Georgian Folk Tales* (London: Abela Publishing, 2009). ISBN 9781907256127. 200 pp.

The Helpful Animals (Burma)

Motif: B350

"The Grateful Beasts" on page 115 in Frances Carpenter, *The Elephant's Bathtub: Wonder Tales from the Far East* (Garden City, NY: Doubleday, 1962). LCCN 62016499. 219 pp.

"The Cat, the Dog, and the Mongoose" on page 52 in Frances Carpenter, *Wonder Tales of Dogs and Cats* (Mattituck, NY: Amereon House, 1955). 255 pp.

A variant "The Enchanted Ring" on page 31 in Aleksandr Afanas'ev, *Russian Fairy Tales* (New York: Pantheon Books, 1945). ISBN 0394730909. 672 pp.

The Three Girls and the Johnnycakes (Appalachia, USA)

Motif: 554A

"The Three Girls and the Journey-Cakes" on page 70 in Ruth Stotter, *The Golden Axe and Other Folktales of Compassion and Greed* (Oakland, CA: Regent Press, Typeset/Layout Stotter Press, 1998). ISBN 0943565162. 183 pp.

"The Three Girls and the Journey-Cakes" on page 140 in Marie Campbell, *Tales from the Cloud Walking Country* (Athens, GA: University of Georgia Press, 2000). ISBN 0820321869. 272 pp.

A video rendition from Sea Road School's Channel, *Youtube. 2014.* https://www.youtube.com/watch?v=d_MPdLstjuY (accessed August 18, 2015).

The Queen Bee (Germany)

Motif: 582.2

"The Queen Bee" on page 232 in Jacob and Wilhelm Grimm, *The Complete Fairy Tales of the Brothers Grimm* (New York: Bantam Books, 2003). ISBN 0553382160. 762 pp.

Brothers Grimm. 2003. *The Queen Bee* (Vancouver, B.C.: Simple Read Books). ISBN 0968876846. 24 pp.

Gene Clark. "Folklore and the Faith, Pt. 2: The Queen Bee." *Wiccan Together.* 2013. http://www.wiccantogether.com/profiles/blogs/folklore-the-faith-pt-2-the-queen-bee (accessed August 18, 2015).

The Two Stepsisters (Norway)

Motif: 480A

"The Two Stepsisters" on page 95 in Ruth Stotter, *The Golden Axe and Other Folktales of Compassion and Greed* (Oakland, CA: Regent Press, Typeset/Layout Stotter Press, 1998). ISBN 0943565162. 183 pp.

"The Two Step-Sisters" on page 103 in George Webbe Dasent, Peter Christen Asbjornsen and Jorgen Moe, *A Selection from the Norse Tales for the Use of Children* (Edinburgh: Edmonston and Douglas, 1862). 364 pp.

The Raja's Son and Princess Labam (India)

Motif: B582.2

"How the Raja's Son Won the Princess Labam" on page 583 in Joanna Cole, *Best Loved Folktales of the World* (New York: Knopf Doubleday Publishing Group, 1982). ISBN 9780385189491. 812 pp.

"How the Raja's Son Won the Princess Labam" on page 3 in Joseph Jacobs, *Indian Fairy Tales* (New York: Dover Publications, Inc., 2011). ISBN 0486218287. 288 pp.

"How the Raja's Son Won the Princess Labam" on page 153 in Maive S. H. Stokes, *Indian Fairy Tales* (Whitefish, MT: Kessinger Publishing Company, 2006). ISBN 9781428628489. 340 pp.

General Dog and His Army (Croatia)

Motif: B571.3

"'General' Dog and His Army" on page 245 in Frances Carpenter, *Wonder Tales of Dogs and Cats* (Mattituck, NY: Amereon, Limited, 1996). ISBN 9780848809454. 255 pp.

A variant of the story, "The Friendly Animals" on page 164 in Ruth Manning-Sanders, *The Book of Magical Beasts* (New York: Thomas Nelson, Inc., 1970). ISBN 0840760086. 244 pp.

Section 5: Creatures of the Imagination

The Boy Who Drew Cats (Japan)

Motif: D435.2.1.1

"The Boy Who Had to Draw Cats" on page 195 in Frances Carpenter, *Wonder Tales of Dogs and Cats* (Mattituck, NY: Amereon House, 1955). 255 pp.

"The Boy Who Drew Cats" on page 113 in Heather Forest, *Wonder Tales from around the World* (Little Rock, AR: August House Publishers, Inc., 1995). ISBN 0874834228. 155 pp.

"The Boy Who Drew Cats" on page 85 by Rafe Martin in Jennifer Justice, ed., *The Ghost and I* (Cambridge, MA: Yellow Moon Press, 1992). ISBN 0938756370. 126 pp.

In Lacadio Hearn, Translator, *Japanese Fairy Tales: The Boy Who Drew Cats* (New York: Cosimo Classics, 2007). ISBN 9781602060715. 136 pp.

The Seal Hunter and the Merman (Scotland)

Motif: B389.1

"The Seal Catcher's Adventure" on page 191 in Sir George Douglas, *Scottish Fairy and Folk Tales* (Mineloa, NY: Dover Publications, 2000). ISBN 0486411400. 360 pp.

"The Seal Catcher and the Merman" on page 63 in Augusta Baker, *The Talking Tree: Fairy Tales from Fifteen Lands* (New York: J.B. Lippincott & Company, 1955). LCCN 55009507. 255 pp.

The Dragons of Ha Long Bay (Vietnam)

Motif: B11.11. 5

"Ha Long-By of Descending Dragons." VEN Productions. 1997–2003. http://www.vietscape.com/travel/halong/index.html (accessed August 18, 2015).

Igor I. Solar. "Vietnam's Vinh Ha Long: the 'Bay of the Descending Dragon.'" *Digital Journal.* 2010. http://www.digitaljournal.com/article/299137 (accessed August 18, 2015).

In 2013, I went to Vietnam on a tour with Indochina Pioneer, Co. Our tour guide was Le Sy Quyen. I prompted him to tell me the local folktales and his version of the Ha Long Bay legend differs from web versions. When the dragons died, their serpentine bodies formed the rocky crags and jagged mountain range surrounding the inlet. I included his version here.

The Leshi Cat (Russia)

Motif: B580

"The Leeshy Cat" on page 37 in Ruth Manning-Sanders, *A Book of Cats and Creatures* (New York: E. P. Dutton, 1981). ISBN 0525267735. 127 pp.

Additional information in Linda J. Ivanits, *Russian Folk Belief* (Armonk, NY: M. E. Sharpe, 1989) and in William Francis Ryan, *The Bathhouse at Midnight: An Historical Survey of Magic and Divination in Russia* (Philadelphia, PA: Pennsylvania State University Press, 1999).

A variant called "The Snake-Peri and the Magic Mirror" on page 257 in Ignacz Kuno, ed., *Four-Four Turkish Fairy Tales* (Berkshire, England: Abela Publishing, 2010). ISBN 1907256377. 476 pp.

Damian and the Dragon (Greece)

Motif: B11.6.1

"Damian and the Dragon" on page 1 in Ruth Manning-Sanders, *Damian and the Dragon* (New York: Roy Publishers, 1965). LCCN 65024641. 190 pp.

"The Dream of the King's Son" on page 322 in Woislav M. Petrovitch, *Hero Tales and Legends of the Serbians* (London: George Harrap & Company, 1921). 394 pp.

Zal, the White Haired (Ancient Persia)

Motif: B535.06

"Zal the White Haired" on page 28 in Barbara Leonie Picard, *Tales of Ancient Persia* (Oxford, England: Oxford University Press, 1993). ISBN 0192741543. 173 pp.

"Zal the White Haired" on page 2 in Rohini Chowdhury, *The Three Princes of Persia* (New York: Penguin Books, 2005). ISBN 014333493X. 176 pp.

The Grateful Fox Fairy (China)

Motif: B651.1.2

"The Grateful Fox Fairy" on page 89 in Frances Carpenter, *Tales of a Chinese Grandmother* (New York: Doubleday, Doran & Company, Inc., 1944). 261 pp.

A variant of the theme is "The Divided Daughter" on page 152 in Moss Roberts, *Chinese Fairy Tales and Fantasies* (New York: Pantheon, 1979). ISBN 039442039X. 259 pp.

The Gift of the Unicorn (China)

Motif: B498

"The Gift of the Unicorn" on page 89 in Joe Nigg, *Wonder Beasts: Tales & Lore of the Phoenix, the Griffin, the Unicorn & the Dragon* (Englewood, CO: Libraries Unlimited, 1995). ISBN 156308242X. 160 pp.

"The Gift of the Unicorn" in Robert Wyndham, *Tales the People Tell in China* (New York: Julian Messner, a division of Simon & Schuster, 1971). ISBN 0671324276.

Section 6: Not One or the Other

Why Platypus Is Special (Australian Aborigines)

Motif: A2300

"Why Platypus Is Such a Special Creature" on page 26 of James Vance Marshall and Francis Firebrace, *Stories from the Billabong* (London: Frances Lincoln Children's Books, 2008). ISBN 9781845077044.

"The Flood and Its Results" on page 163 of W. Ramsay Smith, *Myths & Legends of the Australian Aborigines* (Mineola, NY: Dover Publications, 2003). ISBN 9780486427096.

Questions and Activities

General Discussion Questions
People and Culture

What did the story teach you about the people that live in that part of the world?

Compare and contrast your culture today with the story culture in its time and setting.

What are the social classes in the story and how do they compare to present hierarchy?

What type of houses did they live in?

What kind of clothes did they wear?

What did the people value? Gold? Friendship?

Animals

What did the story teach you about the animals in each story?

What did the animals eat or what would they eat?

Where did they live? Are these animals found in other places or countries?

How did the environment impact the story and the character's behavior?

Describe the physical attributes of the animals in the story.

What virtues did the animals display? Kindness, courage, loyalty, etc.?

Environment

How would the tale change if the story took place in another type of climate or environment? Another culture?

If the story took place in a different climate or environment, would the animals in the story be the same or different, and if different, what animals would be present? How would this difference impact or change the story? What type of foods would these new animals eat? What new talents would be displayed by these different animals?

Discuss the geography of the country of the story's origin.

What new challenges or obstacles would the animals and their human companions face based on a different environment, climate, etc.?

Vocabulary and Language

Have the students mark down all the vocabulary words that are new to them.

Could they understand the meaning of the words through their context in the story?

Could the students replace the word with another word that would say the same thing (synonym)? For example, what word could they use to replace the word samurai?

Have the students brainstorm synonyms and antonyms from their vocabulary words.

Take three or four new vocabulary words as prompts that students may use to create their own story.

Story Structure

Have students tell the story from a different perspective. Tell it from the animal's point of view.

Did the tale remind the students of a story they had already read or heard?

Have the students use the story they read and dramatize it with each student taking a role as an animal, person, or even a magical object like sword or wand.

Write a new ending to the story.

Write a new story based on the one you read but in your neighborhood with your family, friends, and pets.

Write lyrics for a song based on the story.

Specific Story Discussion Questions and Related Activities

Section 1: Creatures of the Land

The Grateful Wolf

Questions:

1. Wolves are shy creatures and mainly hunt weaker animals like rabbits or sometimes sick animals or older animals in herds such as deer or elk. Report a few true statements about wolves and a few false statements about wolves.

2. What do you think might have caused people in the West to see wolves as evil and those in the East to see wolves as more benevolent?

Activity:

Play a game like *Jeopardy* where the class is divided up into teams. Think of an assortment of questions about land mammals such as the fox, wolf, badger, bear, etc. Have each team select a category and then answer the question in the form of a question. Example:

What animal hunts in packs? Answer: "What is a wolf?"

The Maiden and the Puma

Questions:

1. What lives and grows in the pampas? In the United States, is there an ecological area that is similar to the pampas? Support your statement.

   http://www.blueplanetbiomes.org/pampas.htm

2. Was Maldonado a heroine? Why or why not? Can you be a hero or heroine if you disobey orders?

3. Can you find other towns named after famous heroes or heroines?

Activity:

The Ombu is a tree special to South America and the pampas. Have the students select three trees unique to three different regions around the world. Ask them to draw, as accurately as possible, the three trees on three separate sheets of paper. Then list for each tree: how it serves as habitat for other living creatures; its economic value, if any; and statistics of its fruit, height, and size, etc. Have them share their research with the class.

Oleshek, the Deer with the Golden Antlers

Questions:

1. What does the clay man represent in the story?

2. Describe the climate and the environment of the arctic tundra.

Activity:

Show the students examples of Sami art (https://www.flickr.com/photos/jakobeep/8528257049/in/photostream/).

Ask them to create a strip of Sami folk art based on the designs that often were used to border their clothing or other useful articles.

OR

Let the students listen to a traditional Sami song or *joik*, an improvised song.

https://www.youtube.com/watch?v=COJrjvp6JIM

Compare and contrast it to our current folk music.

The Man and the Muskrat

Questions:

1. What countries are neighbors to Tanzania?

2. Why did the hunter think the rat could not possibly help him?

3. Can you think of other stories where small animals defeat larger ones? How do they accomplish this?

Activity:

Research the animals of a different part of the world and write a story about how a small animal helps a larger one.

The Thankful Badger Family

Questions:

1. Like China, early Japan engaged in animal worship. The badger is treated with honor and superstitious awe. In the United States, we have designated the bald eagle as our national bird to symbolize our country. How is this like the Asian attitude toward select animals? Compare and contrast this idea. Think about badgers representing sport teams.

Activity:

Have the students make a list of ten animals in one column. In the next column (column two), ask them to list the physical attributes of each animal. In the last column (column three), have them brainstorm characteristics based on the animal's behavior and the column two attributes. Discuss how people anthropomorphize (giving human characteristics to an animal) animals and how cultures (Native American, for example) used these characteristics to create animal totems.

The Brahmini and the Mongoose

Questions:

The story takes place near the great Ganges River in India.

1. Name the major waterways or rivers in the following places: United States of America, South America, Northern Africa (Egypt), Western Europe.
2. Find the rivers on the world map.
3. How do these waterways impact humans and the surrounding environment?
4. In the Southwestern United States, do we have an animal who, like the mongoose, fights rattlesnakes? (roadrunner)

Activity:

Have the students draw an outline of the above countries (question number 1) and sketch the rivers in the appropriate locations.

How Man Found a Friend

Questions:

1. What other animals have people domesticated or tamed to assist with people's survival?

   (Camels, oxen, horses, mules, any beast of burden or travel)

2. What does '*once bitten, twice shy*' mean?

3. Name a few ways dogs are helpful to people.

4. Why are dogs called "man's best friend"?

Activity:

Write a *pourquoi* story (how and why story) about one of the following topics:

1. Why snakes have no legs

2. How the elephant got an elongated nose or trunk

3. How the skunk got a white stripe down its back

4. Other things in nature

Mighty Mikko

Questions:

1. The fox, through deceit and murder, gains a wife and riches for Mikko. The peasants of that era wished to improve their social standing and lot in life. How is that different or similar to people today.

2. How do you view the means by which the fox obtained the dragon's castle? Were they justified?

Activity:

Write a short story where a pet helps you obtain a goal. OR draw a storyboard with pictures of your story and tell it to the class.

The Young Man Who Refused to Kill

Questions:

1. What is the difference between animal cruelty and killing to eat?

2. Why did Tashi's father throw the rock at his son? What would you do if you were Tashi's father?

Activity:

Draw a picture of the Tibetan flag and explain the symbolism of the colors and the images. Design a new flag that represents your home, city, state, or an imaginary country. Explain the colors you used and the symbolism of the images.

Snake's Blessing

Questions:

1. Do you think people are born with a fear of snakes? Why or why not?

2. Name a few characteristics of reptiles.

3. How do snakes fit into the ecosystem? What good do they do?

4. How do snakes swallow large prey? Discuss how their anatomy enables them to open their mouths wide.

Activity:

Have the students research the local snakes of their state. Make a poster about a nonvenomous or venomous snake.

Blind Man's Bluff

Questions:

1. How is the game of Blind Man's Bluff important to the story? Why was it played in the dark?

2. How would you outsmart the bear? If you could not see, what other senses would you rely on?

Activity:

Think about the song "Ring around the Rosie" and the actions that go with it. Some children's games can be traced back to earlier times. How do the words and actions reflect the underlying meaning of the effects of the Black Death? Make up another short rhyme for swine flu or another modern disease.

How do people who are blind survive in the world? Read about Helen Keller or another visually impaired person and write a report about her or his story.

The White Spider's Gift

Questions:

1. For the final contest, the chieftain requested exotic gifts. One of the men brought rare animal skins. Why is this competition a good or bad idea?

2. Discuss the crisis with the ivory trade or the decimation of the white rhino for its horn. Why should we protect endangered species?

Activity:

Weaving: Take a rectangular piece of cardboard and cut an equal number of slits along the edges on all four sides, trying to match the cuts to the opposite side. Cut pieces of yarn, ribbon, floss, or thread into lengths about three inches longer than the longer side of the cardboard. With a strand of yarn, place one end (with about an inch overlap) between the slit to hold it and repeat on the direct opposite side. Continue until all the slits have yarn stretched across lengthwise, thus creating the warp. Weaving the weft, or filler thread, can be done with short strands or longer strands. The yarn or thread will be drawn through over one warp thread and then under the next warp thread. The student can use a pencil as a shuttle by taping the yarn to the pencil and weaving it through. Have the students experiment with color and thread thickness to create different effects.

Section 2: Creatures of the Sky

How the Wasp Lost His Voice

Questions:

1. What is a khan?

2. What other insects sting or draw blood?

3. What type of eagle is found in Mongolia?

Activities:

Find other birds that are known for their songs and flying ability and other insects that sting and buzz and rewrite the story using these new characters.

The Birds' Garden

Questions:

1. Where is Kazakhstan?

2. How would you describe the friendship between the farmer and the shepherd?

3. What was wrong with the answers of the other students? What would you have done if you had found the chest of gold?

4. Why is a garden important?

Activities:

Cut out photos of flowers from old magazines or draw pictures of flowers yourself and on a large piece of paper create your own garden.

Maui and the Birds

Questions:

1. How many islands make up the nation of New Zealand?

2. What other adventures did Maui have? How did these adventures help the Polynesian people?

3. Describe the environment of New Zealand? How does it differ from its neighbor Australia?

Activities:

The Maori people traveled the ocean in huge boats. Find information about these boats and draw a picture of one. Then look at a map of the Pacific Ocean and try to trace a trip from New Zealand to some of the other islands in the Pacific.

Marko Kraljevic and the Eagle

Questions:

1. Find Serbia and its neighbors on the map. Read about the white-tailed eagle, indigenous to the Balkans.

2. What was important about the Battle of Kosovo?

3. Do you know of any other stories about animals nursing people back to health? What would you have done if you found a wounded eagle?

Activities:

Make a list of the names of other heroes in other countries. Discover if they had animal helpers, and if not, what animal would you imagine they would have as a friend or helper?

The Man, the Dove, and the Hawk

Questions:

1. Which animal did you sympathize with the most?

2. Did his friend do the right thing by not making the decision for him?

3. What did he mean by saying "paddle your own boat?"

4. Was there any other decision that could have resulted in satisfying every one?

Activities:

Research Nigeria and find some of the differences between the many ethnic cultures that live there. Draw a picture of some of the houses that different groups live in and the various types of ethnic dress they wear.

Crane Child

Questions:

1. Do you think it was right for the old man to free the bird caught in another man's trap? Would you have done it?

2. Why did the old couple sneak a peek at the girl while she was weaving? Have you ever wanted to see something you were not supposed to see?

3. Why did the crane girl come to the old couple's home? Why do you think the crane girl had to leave?

Activities:

Make an origami crane: http://www.origami-instructions.com/origami
-crane.html

Tell the Crane Child story to a friend as you make the paper crane.

The Pheasants and the Bell

Questions:

1. Is it right to interfere with nature? Would it be right for you to scare away a fox from eating a baby rabbit?

2. What other animal could have threatened those eggs?

3. Describe the Korean landmass. What state in America does it resemble?

Activities:

Choose a bird that you have seen in your area and then find a description of its nest and build them out of twigs, straw, and other materials.

The Waiting Maid and the Parrot

Questions:

1. Why is the parrot perfect for its role in this story?

2. Have you ever seen a live parrot? Did it talk to you?

3. What other birds are known for their intelligence?

Activities:

In the story the parrot acts as a messenger. Divide the class into two groups. This is a slightly different variation of the game called "telephone." Give each group the same message. Tell the first student the message and then have them whisper it to the next student, sending the message down the line. When the message finally comes to the end of each line, compare how each group conveyed the message. Which group was closest to the original? Which group could have been trusted to be the "parrot" in the story?

The Rooster and the Sultan

Questions:

1. What does the title "sultan" mean?

2. Why was the rooster so angry with the sultan?

3. The rooster would not give up—what do we call this virtue? What does the rooster have that makes him a perfect animal to punish the sultan?

Activities:

Make a list of other animals found on a farm that could have helped the old woman. Make sure you tell us what special talents or physical attributes they have that would help them complete the task.

Yogodayu and the Army of Bees

Questions:

1. How is the bee's stinger like a samurai sword?

2. What do you think made the bees want to help Yogodayu?

3. Could Yogodayu have won the battle without the bees' help? Can you think of another way the bees might have helped Yogodayu win the battle?

Activities:

Make a poster about the bee and list all the positive things they do to help people and the earth. Find pictures of a samurai castle and draw your own version of a castle that is under attack by the bee warriors.

Section 3: Creatures of the Water

The Samurai and the Sea Turtle

Questions

1. What type of land mass is Japan? What parts of this story helped you make your decision?

2. What is a pilgrimage?

3. Why did the young man free the turtle? What would you have done?

4. Does this story remind you of any other stories you already have heard or read? If so, which stories and why?

Activities

Find out what other cultures call their warriors. How would this story change if it were in a land-locked country? What would you need to change in the story? Look up samurai and find how they dressed. Draw a picture of a samurai. What was their symbol of their social rank?

Frog Princess

Questions:

1. In the story the king, his sons, and the wizard were left on a deserted island. How would you have punished them?

2. Vinko was kind, but which character came up with a solution to every problem?

Activities:

Croatia lies on the Balkan Peninsula. Find the other countries that share this area with Croatia. OR As a group, imagine other hard tasks the wizard could come up with and solutions the frog mother would use to defeat him.

Arion and the Dolphin

Questions:

1. Who was the Greek god of the sea?

2. What is a lyre?

3. When you listened to music, did it ever make you want to laugh or cry, or dance and sing along?

Activities:

Find Greece and Sicily on a map and trace the route that Arion might have taken on his journey.

As a group write a song about Arion's adventures.

The Golden Crab

Questions:

1. Why do you think the prince could change into an eagle or a man?

2. In the story, why was the prince bewitched into the form of a crab? Hint: Think about where the country of Greece is located.

3. Why do you think the prince threw the princess, his wife, an apple instead of something else?

Activity:

Draw a picture of the constellation of Cancer. Does it look like a crab? Where is it located? Where is the Big Dipper? Find a picture of the stars in the sky and see how many constellations you can identify.

The Fisherman and His Wife

Questions:

1. What does the story tell us about the lives of poor people at this point in history?

2. Why was the wife never satisfied and always wanting more?

3. Why did the fish finally send the fisherman and his wife back to their old hut? How would you feel if you were constantly told to go back and ask the fish for more wealth?

Activities:

What would you have wished for and why? Think of a different magical animal and write a little poem to it like the one the fisherman used to call the flounder. In one Russian version of this story the fisherman is a woodsman and a tree grants him the wishes because he chose not to cut it down. Describe other occupations a man or woman could have and the animal or creature that would grant the wishes. What might those wishes be?

Emelya, the Fool

Questions:

1. Do you think that Emelya used the power the pike gave him wisely?

2. What would you do if a fish you caught talked to you? If you were given three wishes by the pike, what would they be?

3. Did Emelya gain any wisdom by the end of the story? If not wisdom, what did he gain?

Activities:

In Russia, the ruler is called a tsar. Look up other countries and see what they called their rulers in the past.

The Little Red Fish and the Clog of Gold

Questions:

1. Why did the stepmother hate her stepdaughter so much?

2. What is an arranged marriage?

3. Why didn't the potions work on the fisherman's daughter?

Activities:

The clog is an open-backed, slip-on shoe worn in the Middle East. Relocate the story in another country and find the type of shoes that would be worn there. Find some temporary stick-on tattoos and recreate the henna party.

The Grateful Alligators

Questions:

1. What is the difference between an alligator and a crocodile?

2. Where do crocodiles live? Do these creatures only live in fresh water? Why do alligators and crocodiles only live in warmer climates?

3. What do alligators and crocodiles eat?

Activities:

Draw a picture of a Mississippi riverboat. Find a map and locate the rivers that connect to the Mississippi. Trace the routes a riverboat might have taken from various river cities to New Orleans.

Section 4: Creatures Working Together

The Youth Who Made Friends with the Beasts and the Birds

Questions:

1. Why does the brother-in-law wish to be rid of Huathlacuri?

2. Why does Huathlacuri transform his brother-in-law into a deer instead of a stone or other animal? What does a deer symbolize?

Activities:

The Inca civilization was highly developed. Its art work is distinctive. Have the students research some of the artifacts of the Incas. Look at patterns and drawings. Compare them with modern weaving patterns and art work. Watch a YouTube video about Peru or their native dances.

https://www.youtube.com/watch?v=DEI9UW_zVU4

The King's Youngest Son

Questions:

1. Why was Tholiorko special?

2. Was it wrong for Tholiorko to save the fish's life and not his father's eye sight? What would you do?

Activities:

Draw the flag of the Republic of Georgia as well as the flags of the following countries that surround the Republic of Georgia: Russia, Turkey, Armenia, and Azerbaijan. What do the symbols and colors of the flags mean?

The Helpful Animals

Questions:

1. What does Po learn as a result of his journey?

2. Why didn't his mother manage the property and wealth? Who owned it?

Activity:

Select 12–16 vocabulary words. Pass out graph papers. Have the students create a crossword puzzle using the vocabulary words. Have the students find the antonyms to these words. Incorporate some of these words into the crossword puzzle. Example: lustrous/dull

The Three Girls and the Johnnycakes
Questions:

1. What modern snacks do you take with you when you travel? Do the snacks have a lot of sugar, fat, or salt in them? What are healthy snacks? Are they convenient for travel?

2. Give at least two reasons why Mary was successful in earning the reward. How have friends, family, or other people helped you with a project or task? What have you done for them in return?

Activity:

The teacher will make a johnnycake and bring it to class. The students will bring a family recipe of their favorite snack or food. They may also bring a sample. Share the food items and discuss cultural or regional foods. Put the recipes together for a class cookbook. Cuban storyteller Olga Loya once said that as an immigrant all she and her family brought to the United States was their recipes and their stories.

The Queen Bee
Questions

1. What are the characteristics of insects? Is a spider an insect? Why or why not?

2. Wilford goes against his brothers in protecting the ants, ducks, and bees. Doing the right thing is not always popular. Can you give examples from your experience of a time when you did not go along with the group because it was wrong? Example: cheating, stealing, lying, etc.

Activity:

Draw a picture of a bumblebee. Name the three parts of the insect's body. Show where pollen is collected.

The Two Stepsisters
Questions:

1. What do you think the red color of the box signified?

2. What do you think was in the green box?

3. Do you think the mother's daughter disliked nature? Is that why she was mean to the animals who asked for her help? Have you ever been afraid of the woods or animals in the woods like spiders or chipmunks?

Activities:

Ask the students to rewrite the story in a modern setting, like in a suburb or small town. What animals might the girls meet? Have the students form groups of 8–10 people and devise a play to act out the story with the updated characters.

OR

Have the students list types of trolls (e.g., forest, giant, dwarf, cliff, sea, or gnome-type trolls) and draw pictures of them. Have them assign characteristics of the trolls based on their habitat. What would an American city troll be like? Have the students write a short story based on their troll creation and using their drawings to create a graphic tale.

The Raja's Son and Princess Labam

Questions:

1. Would you say the prince won the hand of Princess Labam fairly?

2. Was it okay that he tricked the four fakirs and took their magical items? Why or why not?

3. Did the prince have magic of his own? What magic did Princess Labam possess?

Activity:

With a partner, have one of the students in the pair come up with a reasonable task or challenge that an animal helper can do to aid a human. The task must be something an animal is capable of doing. The other student of the pair must come up with an animal or animals that can do the task. Create a story that includes how the main character wins the favor of the animal helper(s) who later assists the protagonist. Remember to have a beginning, middle, and end to the story. Tell the story to the class.

General Dog and His Army

Questions:

1. There was a lot of magic in this story. List some of the magical things that happened.

2. How did the army of animals differ from the army of men?

3. If this story happened in America, what different types of animals might have helped Branko? What if it happened in Africa or the Amazon jungle?

Activity:

Create your own animal army. Make masks for each animal and decide what they will do to stop the invading army.

Section 5: Creatures of the Imagination

The Boy Who Drew Cats

Questions:

1. This story took place in old Japan where families had to produce their own food. A fear for them was lack of food or a famine. The rat goblin personifies that fear by devouring the crops and leaving the people starving. How would you personify or symbolize a modern threat or challenge to daily life?

2. In the story, Tomo is not big enough or strong enough to help with farming, yet through his unique talent, he conquers one of the farmers' biggest threats, that of rodents damaging and eating the crops as well as threatening young children. What does this say about individuals approaching problems from a different mind-set or perspective? Do we listen to those who think differently? There are many solutions to a problem, not just one.

Activities:

Some forms of Japanese arts use simple lines to imply images. For example, a couple of "V" strokes in the horizon would represent birds flying. A serpentine line may represent a stream or river. Have the students draw a landscape, figure, or character using a minimal number of strokes of a brush or pen to suggest the scene.

OR

A variation of that idea would be to create a face or figure using the numbers ranging from zero to nine. For example, use the number eight in a horizontal fashion to depict glasses on a face. This is similar to ASCII art, but the artist has the flexibility of moving the numbers in a nonlinear fashion.

The Seal Hunter and the Merman

Questions:

1. Find more tales of mermaids and mermen in other cultures. Why do you think that they are often associated with seals? What other animals are often mistaken as mermaids by sailors? What other cultures have animals that can turn into humans?

2. What did the seal people teach the hunter that made him stop killing seals?

Activities:

What other animals are killed in the ocean needlessly? Research whale hunting and why it continues. What do we need to do to stop hunting sea animals?

Can you write a story about how a whale teaches a hunter not to hunt whales? Do you ever step on ants and other bugs without thinking? How can you stop?

Make up a story about a creature that can turn from animal to human and can be found in your backyard.

The Dragons of Ha Long Bay

Questions:

1. Why do you think that dragons are viewed as friendly and helpful in Eastern cultures but fearsome and threatening in Western cultures? Name a few dragons in literature, songs, or visual media.

2. There are real dragons in the world. Where do they live? (Komodo dragon of Indonesian Islands such as Komodo)

Activity:

Draw pictures of Eastern dragons in their elemental settings (e.g., Asian dragons are associated with water) and Western dragons in their elemental settings (e.g., European dragons live in caves and are associated with fire).

OR have the students create a one-page snapshot about a dragon of their choice.

The Leshi Cat

Questions:

1. In the beginning of the story, Dmitry chose to help the Leshi. What would you do in similar circumstances? Have you ever had to choose between friends or sides of an argument? Give examples.

2. One could argue that the Leshi's offer of friendship represented humans' peaceful coexistence with nature and the land while the devil's offer of gold might represent business profits at the expense of our natural resources. What similar modern day challenges and issues face us? Think about the Deepwater Horizon Oil Spill in the Gulf of Mexico disaster. Which side would you choose in the Keystone Pipeline debate?

Activity:

Assign a research project where the students investigate the environment versus big business activities. OR set up debate teams to argue two sides of an issue such as climate change.

Damian and the Dragon

Questions:

1. Dragons in European folktales are usually fierce and not friendly to people but in this story the dragon adopts Damian as his son. What are the reasons that the dragon treats Damian differently? Would we treat each other differently if we could not see each other?

2. What are the virtues of the dragon that make Damian a better man? What does the dragon teach Damian about family?

Activities:

Blindfold one student and then have another student be their eyes. Have the students guide their blindfolded classmate to the lunchroom, help them with their food, find a place to sit, and guide them back to class. Have each student write about the experience of being blind and about being a guide.

Zal, the White Haired

Questions:

1. Zal was made an outcast by his father because of the color of his hair. Do we still make people feel bad because of the way they look? Why? How can we stop this behavior?

2. How could you tell that the great bird loved Zal? What gift did she give him? Do you think he ever used the gift?

Activities:

Draw a picture of Zal riding the great bird. Show the nest where they lived. Write a story about an adventure that Zal could have with his adopted mother.

The Grateful Fox Fairy

Questions:

1. Foxes have very successfully adapted to the changes in their environment brought on by humans. What are the general characteristics of foxes?

2. What fox characteristics do humans admire or observe. How do people anthropomorphize the fox? Does it differ by culture?

Activities:

Look at a picture of a fox. How does its unique body aid in its survival? Create a new creature with specific features that would help it survive in an urban environment; in a forest. Working in groups of three, take a sheet of paper and fold it to create three spaces. Each student will draw a part of the new creature. The first student will draw the upper portion and then fold the paper so the next student cannot see what was drawn; the second student fills in the middle section and then folds the paper so the third student cannot see the first two drawings. When all three drawings are complete, unfold the paper to see the new creature and discuss if it could survive in the wild or as a pet. (This is similar to the Surrealists activity of the "exquisite corpse.")

The Gift of the Unicorn

Questions:

1. In every culture the unicorn is magical. In this story, he is able to grant a wish. What other magical powers could a unicorn have that would be helpful to people?

2. Look up Confucius and talk about his life and his achievements in China. What were his influences on his country and its rulers? Is he still influential today? Why?

Activities:

The Chinese unicorn is described in the story as being made up of different animal parts and different colors. Draw a picture of the Chinese unicorn. Think of all the positive qualities of different animals and make a list. From that list, construct your own unicorn using the positive attributes of the animals and representing them through the various parts of the animal.

Section 6: Not One or the Other

Why Platypus Is Special

Questions:

1. What is a billabong?

2. Find a picture of a platypus and describe him to your classmates by using other animals. For example: webbed feet like a duck, etc.

3. What other unusual animals are native to Australia?

4. What other islands are also nations?

5. Is the message of platypus important today in our world? Why?

Activities:

Have each member of the class find one thing about himself or herself that is unique. Share it with the class and see how we can all appreciate each other's differences.

OR

Find other animals that are both unique to one area of the world and also in appearance. Draw a picture of the animal and present a report to the class.

Bibliography

Story Collections

Bruchac, Joseph. 1992. *Native American Animal Stories*. Golden, CO: Fulcrum Publishing. ISBN 1555911277.

Bruchac, Joseph. 1995. *Dog People: Native Dog Stories*. Golden, CO: Fulcrum Publishing. ISBN 1555912281.

Climo, Shirley. 2005. *Monkey Business: Stories from around the World*. New York: Henry Holt & Company. ISBN 9780805063929.

Cole, Joanna. 1983. *Best-Loved Folktales of the World*. Garden City, NY: Anchor Books. ISBN 0385189494.

Dean, Jana. *Wetland Tales: A Collection of Stories for Wetland Education*. Olympia, WA: Publications Office, Department of Ecology, Publication #92-17.

DeSpain, Pleasant. 1994. *Eleven Turtle Tales: Adventure Tales from around the World*. Little Rock, AR: August House. ISBN 0874833884.

DeSpain, Pleasant. 1996. *Eleven Nature Tales: A Multicultural Journey*. Little Rock, AR: August House. ISBN 0874834589.

Ferguson, Gary. 1997. *Spirits of the World: The World's Great Nature Myths*. New York: Three Rivers Press. ISBN 0609801430.

Gaster, Moses. 1915. *Rumanian Bird and Beast Stories.* White Fish, MT: (Originally published by The Folk-Lore Society) reprinted by Kessinger Publishing. ISBN 0766149021.

Green, Roger Lancelyn. 1970. *The Hamish Hamilton Book of Dragons.* London: Hamish Hamilton. ISBN 0809824132.

Green, Thomas A. 2006. *The Greenwood Library of American Folktales, Four Volumes.* Westport, CT: Greenwood Press. ISBN 0313337721 (set).

Green, Thomas A. 2008. *The Greenwood Library of World Folktales, Four Volumes.* Westport, CT: Greenwood Press. ISBN 9780313337833 (set).

Haney, Jack V. 1999. *Russian Animal Tales.* Armonk, NY: M.E. Sharpe. ISBN 156324490X.

Harris, Rosemary. 1974. *Sea Magic & Other Stories of Enchantment.* New York: Macmillan Publishing. ISBN 0027426505.

Hausman, Gerald and Loretta. 1999. *Dogs of Myth: Tales from around the World.* New York: Simon & Schuster. ISBN 0689806965.

Hill, Craig. 2008. *The Complete Fables of La Fontaine.* New York: Arcade Publishing. ISBN 9781611453447.

Hodges, Margaret. 1984. *If You Had a Horse: Steeds of Myth & Legend.* New York: Charles Scribner's Sons. ISBN 0684182202.

Hoffman, Mary. 1998. *A Twist in the Tail: Animal Stories from around the World.* New York: Henry Holt & Company. ISBN 0805059466.

Keding, Dan. 2008. *Elder Tales: Stories of Wisdom & Courage from around the World.* Westport, CT: Libraries Unlimited. ISBN 9781591585947.

Keding, Dan. 2010a. *The United States of Storytelling: Folktales & True Stories from the Eastern States.* Santa Barbara, CA: Libraries Unlimited. ISBN 9781591587279.

Keding, Dan. 2010b. *The United States of Storytelling: Folktales & True Stories from the Western States.* Santa Barbara, CA: Libraries Unlimited. ISBN 9781591587286.

Kritsky, Gene and Cherry, Ron. 2000. *Insect Mythology.* New York: Writers Club Press. ISBN 0595150179.

Lester, Julius. 1999. *Uncle Remus: The Complete Tales.* New York: Phyllis Fogelman Books. ISBN 0803724519.

McNamee, Gregory. 2000. *The Serpent's Tale: Snakes in Folklore & Literature*. Athens, GA: The University of Georgia Press. ISBN 0820322253.

Norman, Howard. 2004. *Between Heaven & Earth: Bird Tales from around the World*. New York: Gulliver Books. ISBN 0152019820.

Perrin, Pat. 2010. *Horses: In Myth, Legends, Folktales & Other Ancient Stories*. Laconia, NH: Madeira Myth Collections. ISBN 9781 935178149.

Russell, Randy. 2008. *Ghost Cats of the South*. Winston-Salem, NC: John F. Blair Publisher. ISBN 9780895873606.

Russell, Randy and Barnett, Janet. 2001. *Ghost Dogs of the South*. Winston-Salem, NC: John F. Blair Publisher. ISBN 0895872889.

Stephens, John Richard. 2009. *The King of Cats & Other Feline Fairy Tales*. New York: Fall River Press. ISBN 9781435115873.

Tate, Peter. 2007. *Flights of Fancy: Birds in Myth, Legend, and Superstition*. New York: Delacorte Press. ISBN 9780385342483.

Terada, Alice M. 1994. *The Magic Crocodile & Other Folktales from Indonesia*. Honolulu, HI: University of Hawaii Press. ISBN 0824816544.

Yolen, Jane. 1982. *Neptune Rising: Songs and Tales of the Undersea Folk*. New York: Philomel Books. ISBN 0399209182.

Yolen, Jane. 1986. *Favorite Folktales from around the World*. New York: Pantheon Books. ISBN 0613181042.

Nature

Andrews, Tamra. 1998. *Legends of the Earth, Sea and Sky: An Encyclopedia of Nature Myths*. Santa Barbara, CA: ABC-CLIO. ISBN 0874369630.

Bierhorst, John. 1994. *The Way of the Earth: Native Americans and the Environment*. New York: William Morrow & Company. ISBN 0688115608.

Caduto, Michael and Bruchac, Joseph. 1997. *Keepers of the Animals*. Golden, CO: Fulcrum Publishing. ISBN 1555910882.

Klepac, Ariana. 2008. *The Whales Companion*. London: Murdoch Books. ISBN 9781741960402.

Strauss, Kevin. 2006. *Tales with Tails.* Westport, CT: Libraries Unlimited. ISBN 1591582695.

History

Allen, W. E. D. 1932. *A History of the Georgian People.* London: Kegan Paul. Reprint 1971.

Gardanova, B. A., et al., eds. 1962. *Narody Kavkaza* (The Peoples of the Caucasus). Vol. 2. Moscow: Akademiia Nauk.

Lloyd, John and John Mitchinson. 2007. *The Book of Animal Ignorance: Everything You Think You Know Is Wrong.* New York: Harmony Books. ISBN 9780307394934.

Niles, Doug. 2013. *Dragons: The Myths, Legends and Lore.* Avon, MA: Adams Media. ISBN 1440562156.

Opie, Peter and Iona. 1984. *Children's Games in Street and Playground.* Oxford, England: Oxford University Press. ISBN 0192814893.

Web Sites

McCaffrey, Joyce. "Trolls: Culture and Development." *CCB, Library of Information Sciences, University of Illinois,* http://ccb.lis.illinois.edu/ Projects/storytelling/jvmccaff/types1.html (accessed September 21, 2015).

Schaffner, Brynn. "The Pampas." *Blue Planet Biomes.* http://www.blue planetbiomes.org/pampas.htm (accessed September 21, 2015).

Windsor, Brooke. "Trolls-From Ancient to Modern." *Mystic Files,* http://www .mysticfiles.com/trolls-from-ancient-to-modern/ (accessed September 21, 2015).

Index

About the Authors

DAN KEDING serves as adjunct lecturer at the Graduate School of Library and Information Sciences at the University of Illinois, Urbana-Champaign, and performs as a storyteller, author, and folk musician. His published works include *Stories of Hope and Spirit: Folktales from Eastern Europe*, a book that received the Anne Izard Storyteller's Choice Award and the Storytelling World Honor Award. Keding also won the National Story-telling Network's Circle of Excellence Award presented for exceptional commitment and exemplary contributions to the art of storytelling.

KATHLEEN A. BRINKMANN is also a spoken word artist, writer, and scholar of folktales. She served as producer and host for UPTV's *The Stories We Tell*, a program of recorded concerts, interviews with authors, and story-tellers, from 2008 to 2012. She is a founding member of the Champaign-Urbana Storytelling Guild in 2001, where she served as secretary, treasurer, and president for several years. She holds a master's degree in folktales and storytelling from the University of Illinois at Springfield.